YOU—ME—US

You are like me, and I am like you. We are all alike, and there is a universality of sameness in all of us. We have the same essential drives and needs. We want to feel important; we want to feel loved and needed; we want to be close to others. In our efforts to be understood and appreciated we intuitively know that the conduit leading to such a common goal is intimacy. It's something everyone seeks, desires, misses.

Welcome to the Club.

We will send you a free catalog on request. Any titles not in your local book store can be purchased by mail. Send the price of the book plus 35¢ shipping charge to Leisure Books, P.O. Box 270, Norwalk, Connecticut 06852.

Titles currently in print are available for industrial and sales promotion at reduced rates. Address inquiries to Nordon Publications, Inc., Two Park Avenue, New York, New York 10016, Attention: Premium Sales Department.

Dr. Edward Stark's
Intimacy

LEISURE BOOKS • NEW YORK CITY

A LEISURE BOOK

Published by

Nordon Publications, Inc.
Two Park Avenue
New York, N.Y. 10016

Copyright © 1978 by Nordon Publications, Inc.

All rights reserved
Printed in the United States

Intimacy

Foreword

I have been in private practice as a psychoanalyst for almost twenty years. During that time I have been a professional voyeur, a mirror reflecting the painful anguish of the suffering, a listener with a third ear. The analyst is the twentieth century witch doctor to some, the poet of the human condition to others. He offers one major talent: an understanding of the unconscious. And, aware of my own unconscious in the interpersonal "I-thou-here-and-now" which makes up the analytic arena, it has often been apparent that what the patient needs most is a journey into a never-before-experienced-relationship with another human being which was denied him in the world outside. But it was just as apparent that this is not a need reserved for an office, or to be shared only with an analyst. There is a terrible void in all of us for a truly close relationship with those around us. How understandable, then, that the most frequent plea which I hear with that third ear is a plea for intimacy, intimacy, i-n-t-i-m-a-c-y. The cry is so constant, so powerful, so overwhelming, that it reaches the very core of the analytic experience. But is it not a need we *all* feel, a goal we are all seeking? The eyes of Man are sad and lonely. One seeks out another's eyes, and both try to make contact. Why do you always look away at the last moment? If intimacy falls into two categories, sexual and non-sexual, haven't we failed quite dismally to achieve it in both areas?

We even have difficulty defining the word "intimacy." Dictionary definitions are useless: they equate intimacy with small rooms, expertise in a particular discipline, or sexual contact. In the search for definitions of intimacy a major question emerges: Why do men and women find it so hard to communicate? Why do the words "I love you," or "I need you," or "Please let me be close to you"—needs yearning to be expressed, and so often are—fail to bring any measure of intimacy? Many scientific studies show that without such intimacy a vital life force is removed, and the human being simply does not function effectively. Even worse, without it he can go mad; he can die.

Plato once suggested an interesting idea. Originally, the human being was round like a ball, signifying wholeness, and androgynous (the characteristics of both sexes were united). This strange being had four feet, four hands, one neck, and two faces. Everything was double. Possessed of enormous power, these male-female beings attempted to assault the gods. Zeus became angry and split the creatures into two individual parts—male and female. Since then the striving to be reunited is expressed in the longing of each sex for the other so that, as in the former state, they may be as one. This fable is significant when we consider that one of the most urgent—and least understood—needs in the endless quest for compatibility between the sexes, is the need for stronger bonds, an honest relationship, and, yes, that haunting word, intimacy.

"We can't communicate!" I have heard that so often. I heard it said by people who were articulate, educated, sophisticated; people who could use words and mold them carefully and flexibly into understandable ideas. Men and women who were comfortable in the world of the abstract, as well as the real, were pleading for a way to get closer. I listened carefully. I tried to hear the deepest meaning of their words. I pondered on this ever-recurring variation on a theme: If people could talk, talk well, even brilliantly, it did not mean they could communicate.

The patients could communicate on a verbal level. They could speak and understand the words, phrases and sentences. But it didn't seem to satisfy their needs. Somehow that just wasn't enough. It was a band-aid on a gaping wound, a simple cauterizing on a gangrenous sore. So, words weren't enough. Nor, for that matter, was the dazzling intellectual combination of words and ideas enough. What was still missing was a way to establish—or reestablish—a sagging relationship which had once seemed vibrant but which now left the members of the team feeling hollow. Each was reaching out but the stretching arms weren't long enough to make the fingertips touch.

The psychoanalyst is exceedingly comfortable with introspection. Gut-level feelings are his stock-in-trade, his calling card as it were. He recognizes the subtle nuances which distinguish intimacy and communication. He knows that too often we assume that to verbalize effectively assures intimacy. Two simple examples (and there are many) illustrate the fallacy of that premise:

The "con man" in his mastery of greased-lightning interpersonal communication never experiences enough anxiety to care about the victims of his racket, nor enough loving relationships to experience intimacy with the world around him.

The politician, the door-to-door salesman, the used car dealer—indeed, much of the sales power in our mercantile commercial American structure—function effectively through speedy communication talents which never need to establish warmth and love in their interpersonal involvments.

If verbal communication fails to establish the true closeness people want, and if intimacy is seldom achieved in life (including our sex lives), then it must be because people don't want to be understood rationally or on an intellectual level. What seems to be needed is the proper blending of the major formula; the intimate body contact, a loving word, and the emotional chemistry which makes people feel close, cherished, and special. It sounds simple. Why have so few people attained it? The great prophets felt that man *could* attain it.

Disciple: Buddha, are you God?

Buddha: No, I am not God.

Disciple: Are you a priest, Buddha?

Buddha: No, I am not a priest.

Disciple: Well, then Buddha, are you a *teacher*?

Buddha: (Patiently, and with a smile). No, I am not a teacher.

Disciple: (Now impatient and unsmiling). Well, then, what *are* you?

Buddha: I am awake.

Buddha was human, not divine. But he had learned to tune in to all his senses. He knew how to see, hear, touch, and feel what was going on in the world around him. This allowed him to make the ultimate communication with himself, his fellow man, and the Spiritual Universe. Not being divine, he was saying that any man could learn to do the same. It's known as being "in touch," or "with it." It's not mystical, and it's not reserved for a special few.

Helping the reader know how—and why—he has failed to become intimate and comfortable with himself and his world is what this book is all about. Helping the reader to *overcome* the inability to develop intimacy is what this book hopes to achieve.

Preface

It's a tough world out there. It's a snarling, "I'm gonna get mine" society. You're not just part of it. You *are* it.

Sure, you're tired of running scared, feeling frustrated, angry, put upon. Has it ever occurred to you that you are a pretty unintimate person yourself? Who me, you ask? Yes, you. You don't think so. You feel it's *them*. It's the others. You don't know what I'm talking about.

We are so much in the middle of our crazy society that it's become almost comfortable at times and we don't even seem to care about the ugliness all around us. Few of us can communicate adequately with either loved ones or associates. Most of us are terribly afraid, and fear is the cornerstone of all this *un*intimacy. We are afraid of people, afraid of situations, afraid of life.

We have created a society which overwhelms us, which perpetuates our fears. We react to its pressures in unreasonable, unthinking, overemotional and addicted ways.

We are lonely. We lack self-esteem. We lack confidence. We search for true self-awareness, but too often find ourselves sealed off from the world around us. We have been educated (conditioned, programmed) away from a capacity for intimacy. Worst of all, we have become geared towards seeking solutions outside ourselves when both problems and solutions are within.

You may not know who you are, or how to feel loving in this society. Before we finish sharing this book, however, there may emerge the real you—a loving, caring, and potentially intimate you. That is my intention.

Along the way, let's make it our intention to have some fun and even laugh at ourselves as we learn what being intimate is *really* all about.

Where Did All That Loving Go?

Let's play peek-a-boo.

I'll cover my eyes.
You cover your eyes.
Now we can't see anything.
Especially each other.

Let's play peek-a-boo.
Now let's cover our ears.
And our mouths.

I can't move now.

I'll just have to stand here.
Otherwise I'll have to go
Inside myself.

This game isn't so bad.
I'm getting used to it.
Let's change the name
From peek-a-boo.

Let's call this game Society.

Chapter 1

Where Did All That Loving Go?

This is a book about people and society. We can't make it in a society unless we *understand* that society. We can't understand that society unless we know what it takes to cope with that society. Intimacy can't happen unless we first learn to relate to others; and, before that, to know and accept ourselves.

This book is about experiencing. Life is experiencing. Reading this book is experiencing this book; talking about the book, or hearing about it, or wanting to read it can never be the same as experiencing the book itself.

This is also a book about communication. When people can handle their frustrations, when they can be in touch with their experiences at the moment they are experiencing them, they can at least *start* to communicate with others without fear.

This book is dedicated to all the people out there who suffer from a terrible ailment. The diagnosis? They suffer from a terminal case of hardening of the attitudes.

This is a book about intimacy—the intimacy which centers around and grows from a desire to relate on a close level with people. It's also a book about sexual intimacy. There can't be *any* intimacy unless it takes place between two intimate people. Oh yes, there can be sex, there can be screwing, balling, fornication, just plain fucking. But that's not necessarily sexual intimacy. Sexual intimacy is an outgrowth of people-intimacy, and we have to understand what intimacy is composed of first. Making it in our society has to precede making it in bed.

Two friends are talking. They are trying to find what this elusive "thing" called intimacy really is.

It's opening up your insides.
No. That would alienate too many people.
Maybe it starts with good sex.
Without really intimate feelings?
Yes. Like a quickie.

No, you need *time* to develop true intimacy.
That's true.
It's confusing. Let's think about it.
(*a long pause*)

Who do we know who is really intimate?
Let's see. Sandy? Billy? Frank?
(*General agreement that it's not they*).

David has it. And he's only 18.
Yes, I agree. David has it.
You know where you stand with him.
He tells you how he really feels.
(*Both warming up to it now*).
He gives you space. Doesn't crowd you.
And he doesn't dump on you. Rip you.
So why don't we do what David does?
(*a long pause*)

I guess we are afraid we might hurt, or worse, get hurt.
Yeah. To alienate.
I guess we feel the issue isn't enough to...to...
To destroy a friendship.
So that's what brings non-intimacy?
I guess so. Afraid to hurt, afraid to be hurt.

It's so hard.
Yeah, Damned hard.
Even now, thinking of it scares me.
We're intimate because you could tell me that.
I guess so. But if I thought it would hurt you...
Yes? You wouldn't tell me?
Maybe not.
Wow.

What is this strange thing everyone talks about, everybody wants, yet few people can define, and almost nobody feels he or she has: Intimacy?

There are many definitions of intimacy. Here is one I like:

Intimacy is a good feeling,
an almost "ah ha" sensation,
maybe likened to an orgasm in that
we know it when we feel it.

Essentially, it depends on contact.
Close emotional contact between
two or more individuals. Individuals
who can move toward each other without fear.

Without fear of exposing their
weaknesses.
Their inadequacies.

So, intimacy is revealing oneself,
without fear that there is danger
in such exposure.

There are other parameters of intimacy. Intimacy calls for the ability to risk a friendship when it is appropriate. It is being able to reveal some part of one's Self to another. It is attempting to see others in their own uniqueness and not through past experiences.

Intimacy, then, has to be described as a relationship where two people can reveal themselves to one another—and not necessarily their innermost secrets. We are born alone, and we die alone, and there are parts of us which of necessity will always remain embedded within our inner psyche of psyches. And that's all right. For we seem to need that privacy for our integrity. What we want to share, we share. It just calls for some honesty, some trust, some willingness for open talk—without fear.

You are like me, and I am like you. We are all alike, and there is a universality of sameness in all of us. While features and heredity and basic environmental background differ in all of us, we have the same essential drives and needs. We want to feel important; we want to feel loved and needed; we want to be close to others. In our efforts to be understood and appreciated we intuitively know that the conduit leading to such a common goal is intimacy. It's something everyone seeks, desires, misses. Welcome to the Club.

Are you intimate? If you are, you know it. You are one of the few, the lucky minority, the one who probably has close relationships with men and women which satisfy you. You go to others, and have others come to you so that you can engage in some kind of feeling-tinged dialogue. And if you are intimate, a book like this may be confirmation to you of that blessing.

If you are not intimate you may have difficulty extending yourself to those around you. You are probably afraid of people, afraid of too many situations in your daily life—maybe even afraid of life. If you are not intimate you find it hard to communicate; not just superficially, but on a feeling level, revealing yourself to others.

All you have to do is look about you, at your friends, family, business associates, acquaintances, neighbors—and ask yourself if you have an intimate relationship with any *one* of them. And then ask yourself if you are a truly intimate person who invites intimacy. Somewhere it's been written:

> Be willing to happen to somebody,
> And somebody will happen to you.

As an analyst I have become aware that

we seem to have two secret fears: that we are a little crazy, or may go crazy; that we are not really too bright, maybe even a little stupid. Our concern is that if we are not too careful others will discover our secret fears. What wonderful grist for the non-intimate mill!

At the root of non-intimacy is another biggie: lack of trust. Love at first sight is a popular concept. But what occurs is not total trust at first sight. It may be a physical attraction; or associations with other important and pleasant relationships. But before we can trust, a long and gradual sequence of close experiences has to take place. Without trust, we keep our distance. Yet we secretly hope that one enchanted evening we will see a stranger across a crowded room who will become close to us and be a stranger no more.

But what kind of trust are we talking about? What does one person want to entrust with another? We are not talking about material things. We are speaking of the kind of trust which will make one person allow another to *see* what is going on inside, to *hear* how another feels, to touch the inner Self. That's a kind of sensating which is multidimensional and it is difficult, so very difficult to take a chance. Not just with strangers, certainly, but with friends and family as well.

How did we get so traumatized? The

resistance to letting go and trusting is enormous. And yet, without trust, we seem to be simply unprepared for intimacy. As we fear more, trust less, we feel more and more distance and alienation from other human beings.

I spoke with a colleague who worked with NASA and who was involved with the astronauts and the space program. He said:

There were problems.

Lots of them.

Getting them there was a problem.

Bringing them back was another one.

But the biggest problem?

That crushing loneliness.

I understood what he meant. We are isolated from one another, and find enormous conflict in that alienation. Intimacy is not just sentiment. It is part of our survival kit. The need for human closeness has been studied. Babies die without it and adults try to devise more and more ways of attaining it.

It is easy to describe the non-intimate person. That person is not evil; he or she is not bad. That person is simply finding life painful, for the clouds of her or his misperceptions move in front of the sun which is at the core and the center of all of us. The result is lost happiness, for the non-intimate person is simply not living effectively.

The non-intimate person lives in a world

of "them," and "others," and "outsiders." That person focuses and dwells in a world of differences among the people of his world. Such a world is a subject-object world, and it is a bipolar one made of *me* and *them,* or as a famous philosopher said, "I and thou."

If our society is a relentless one, then the non-intimate are at war with others around them. When the world does not supply them with their needs, they feel cheated, for in their perception, the world is their oyster.

Many of us are resentful and unhappy because we're forced to cope with a "world we didn't make." That's a goof-off thinking, because we're almost carbon copies of the people who *did* make it, and we're the ones who are making it today in much the same old ways. *We*, not *they*, are responsible for our present day world. It is the only one we have. Heaven or hell—which will it be?

The non-intimate portion of our society depends upon the realities of life with which it can't cope, to support its rationalizations that it is better off keeping a distance from its fellow man. One of those realities: the world is crowded. The non-intimate see Man moving about in a planet which, as it continues to populate, is less bountiful and yielding for him and his family. Such a man experiences a *people pollution* and all corners of the compass close in on him so that he is increasingly aware of pressures he feels from having to mix, relate, and even depend upon his neighbor.

Once there *was* space to move about, room enough to pick up and move on to new territories and new boundaries if one chose. But the boundaries have closed in, and they have become like the ropes around the boxing ring. Man has discovered, as many a boxer has, that he can run, but he can't hide. Those who can't cope, the non-intimate, find themselves alone in the middle of the arena, isolated and fearful as they warily circle the others. It's a *danse macabre* choreographed by the ultimate non-intimate, and danced out in pantomime by foolish people with unseeing eyes.

We have reached such little intimacy in our society that we have attained the extreme: actual fear of one another. We move away from the people around us, rather than towards them. We see a two-fold population: us and them. The more non-intimate we get in our social interactions, the simpler it is to feel that there are "others" and "outsiders."

When that happens it is difficult to be friendly with strangers, compassionate with acquaintances and truly involved with loved ones. Today, our society stands at arm's length, peering at one another warily, either too concerned with what the next person's move will be, or worse, not really caring at all and oblivious to the other person's existence. We are products of a society which helped turn us out (in varying degrees) as people who are afraid of being rebuffed, afraid of life situations, lonely, uncertain, lacking in self-esteem, lacking in self-awareness, riddled with resentments, wrapped in protective armor (often bristling with spikes), sealed off from the world around us.

Buddha said "I am awake," but *we* are not awake. We don't even *want* to be aware of all that nastiness out there, nor do we want to search out the beauty that truly surrounds us in a bountiful world.

Some men, almost miraculously, have achieved closeness. But what about the rest of us? The unintimate are among us and like the Grim Reaper have created wide, sweeping damage with the scythe of separation and alienation. We'll look at them and see how, in subtle and not-so-subtle ways they creep into our midst and pollute and engulf us with non-intimate behavior.

If *awareness* is the first sign of the possibility of cure, then my hope is to make the reader aware of the ugly scourge surrounding us—non-intimate behavior—and see how it seduces him into similarly addicted ways of behaving. Maybe the next time he sees it operating in his own world, he may reflect, stop, take a good look, and perhaps consider some detour away from the road to alienation. He may have to look rather carefully, but he'll have no trouble *hearing* evidence of it. For it is all around him.

We appear to have a severe language barrier, a barrier within our mother tongue, relating to words we learned to read and write in school since childhood; words we speak and hear every day. This is language we use as we grow up, and as we fit ourselves into various social and professional slots. Instead of language as a form of communication, we seem to be climbing a Tower of Babel, where too often we appear to be addressing each other in foreign tongues. The words are words we all know, but they serve to separate rather than cement relationships. It is the roaring sound known as insult language.

I have long been fascinated by the subtle nuances of the dirty word, the ethnic joke, the humor in our society, and the use of professional jargon—all of which separate us from each other. My theories about them—theories which grew largely from experiences with patients as they revealed their angry feelings to me, coupled with my observations of the world around me—have led me to the examination of words used as barriers to keep us apart.

Insult verbiage is deeply ingrained in our

language. Too many of us find it easier to speak of the Wop, the Kike, the Spick, and the Nigger, than to see them as Italians, Jews, Hispanics, or Blacks. These broad terms serve as wastebaskets for our collective anger and hostility, and are easy short cuts for belching out our feelings of distanciation and unintimacy.

Ethnic diatribes are reserved (as is our humor) for what we fear or dislike, be it a person or an institution. We know that we *are* society, but we resent it frantically. We have become slaves to our own creation—to the thing that is Us, but which we tend to regard as Them. Our helplessness in crowds and our anger towards reciprocal discourtesies leave us hurt by the cruelties we experience, and we think of our fellow beings in terms of masses rather than as individuals. Ultimately they are all potential enemies and outsiders. It is still a world of no trust and aloneness. Our anger is irrational, and our reasoning is unreasonable.

Obscenity is another use of verbalizations which further separate us. When someone says "Go fuck yourself," it's easy to say that powerful communication has taken place. It is shortcut dialogue on the lowest level of consciousness. The word "fuck" has an enormous range of meaning at different times. For some reason men use that word to convey the height of emotion. Women, for some reason, that is not too clear, tend to use the word "shit" when they are upset. It should be pointed out that these words are no longer limited to adults. There was a time when children knew the words but used them as secret passwords to the initiation rites among themselves.

Today, children—even at the elementary level—use these words. This kind of word game, like all games, serves a social purpose. While once shocking and taboo, today's society allows obscenity to provide a socially acceptable projection surface for repressed motives and instinctual needs. It's almost as if we strike some kind of symbolic bargain between our own needs and the norms and rules of society. That's why it falls within the bailiwick of gamesmanship; all games set up bargains and structure in their basic ground rules. When women use it, it can be chic and socially sophisticated; when men use it it is macho and powerful. The sex game is thus acted out in a silent—or verbalized—pantomime.

When we hear obscenity we are also witness to rebellion, for we are present at nose-thumbing at the prevailing establishment. The younger the user of obscenity the more likely that we are hearing the natural idiom of rebellion.

Since we have so many anxieties about

sex and have such difficulty handling our repressed feelings which come out in the substitute form of the joke in our society, it is not surprising that we use the "dirtiest" word of all—fuck—in a peculiar way. We speak of a "fucking tire" when it goes flat; we refer to a "fucking idiot" when we don't like someone; and the "fucking wristwatch" has stopped running. In that way we invest objects with their own sexuality and ascribe sexual activity to inanimate objects, possessions which don't serve us well or people who disappoint or anger us. Thus, in swearing, we infuse sex into an object which has no gender. If, from my own purely personal observation, women use the word "shit" much more than men, they are using a strictly scatalogical term to let off steam. Interestingly, men use sexually-oriented words like "fuck" to attain the same effect. Men also blend the scatalogical and the religious into an emotional "holy shit", a frustration-filled "Jesus Christ," or a "God damned" reference to an object of scorn.

Crude as they are, most four-letter words belong in any examination of communication because they have the virtue of simplicity and directness. Unfortunately they reflect emotional explosiveness rather than an ability to intelligently express something. As a result, they often serve to erect a barrier between people for they serve the user of the four-letter word as a shield against what he feels is a threatening situation.

Even muttering under one's breath is a symbol of human community. They are soft, but they do speak. There certainly is some effort at communicating, for ultimately, no man can speak except to another. Obscenity changes as conditions change, for obscenity is a creature of time and place. Too often, muttering or speaking aloud, the peppering of dialogue with obscenities reflects a laziness to spell out one's emotions in precise terms or an inability to do so. Whether unwilling or unable to be in touch on a true and simple level of communication with one's emotions, the obscenity reflects emotion and passion without explaining or exploring those emotions in depth.

At such times, powerful emotions are rarely spelled out with graceful adjectival verbalizations. When aroused, the expletive serves very well. The listener nods his head, conveying that he understands, follows the trend of the conversation, and is in touch with the speaker and what he is trying to convey. But is he really?

John: "I've been like, er, working at Atlas for like four years, you know?

Jim: Uh huh.

John: And I put in a fuckin' lot of overtime, you know?

Jim: Uh huh.

John: So, this guy, you know who I mean?

Jim: Yeah.

John: He calls me in, and like, that's it. You know?

Jim: Shit! He found out?

John: No. Found out what?

Jim: I don't know. So what was it?

John: He fired me.

Jim: The bastard!

John: I didn't get it, you know?

Jim: (*Silence*)

John: I feel like—you know. What kind of shit is that? I've been working my ass off. Overtime. Everything.

Jim: (*Silence*)

John: He just says "sorry." I told him he could go fuck himself. You know?

Jim: Yeah, Jesus.

John: (*Agitated now, his arms flying, his*

eyes blazing.) I don't know what the hell he pulled that shit on me for.

Jim: Fuck him.

John: I told him he could stuff the job.

Jim: Why'd he fire you?

John: I've been messed up; lots of trouble with...er...you know?

Jim: Oh yeah.

John: I really been freaked out.

Jim: Yeah.

John: Shitty, right?

Jim: You tell him all that?

John: No, fuck him. None of his goddamned business. Like I said, he could stuff the job.

Jim: Yeah.

John: But the bastard coulda told me man-to-man, and leveled with me why he was firing me.

Jim: Yeah, some guys just ain't got no heart or feeling for another guy's problems.

The essence of the conversation: John had been fired, in his estimation, unfairly. John knew only one thing: He was right. The boss was wrong. There was nothing else to talk about. The essence would always be that: John was right. Everthing else then was wrong. And, being right, the boss could "stuff the job." And besides, what was bothering John was "none of his business."

Jim appeared compassionate. He may even have tried to listen. But the meanings behind John's words were convoluted and peppered with shortcuts which he assumed Jim would understand. Do you think Jim understood? Did any communication take place between John and his boss: or for that matter, between John and his friend? On a superficial level, yes. But only superficially—tangentially.

The friendly social interaction, interfered with by the language barriers which employ the expletive and the insult language, also is stopped on a far more subtle, sophisticated level. This level is the professional jargon. How neat to keep others out of our clique, our tight little club, by the simple expedient of using language which only our members know! If you are not a member of the secret club, you are kept at arm's length. The child who sends away three box tops and receives the secret ring, the badge of membership, and now knows the password, has formed an alliance with the other children who have sent away the box tops, have received the secret ring and know that same password. On one level, it's the password used in the army when challenged by the corporal of the guard; the top-secret information possessed by members of the CIA. On another level, it's being able to say "Joe sent me" to the man who peers at you from behind the peephole at the ultra-exclusive club. On a far more mundane level, it appears to infiltrate into many societal and industrial groups. All this verbal gimmickry is used to emphasize separateness through superiority, or expertise in a particular field. Some examples of this clannish jargon:

Electrician: "I want temporary lines hooked up ... Give me a laundry tail on one phase and a left-handed socket on another phase. Use a ten-gauge wire and spread it along the line using a Buchanan for splicing, as well as a crimping tool."

What did he say? "Hook up a temporary power line and screw in a light bulb."

Dentist: "We will have to equilibrate your occlusion to solve your temporal mandibular joint problem."

What did he say? "We will have to correct your bite."

Doctor: "I haven't seen your wife lately."
"Well, she's been in the hospital."
"Oh? I'm so sorry. What was wrong?"
"She had a rhyitidoplasty."
"Goodness. How awful!"
"They also performed a blepharoplasty."
"Oh, God. Is she better?"
"Oh yes. She's home now. She's fine."

What did he say? His wife had a facelift.

Doctor: "You have a pulmonary embolism secondary to chronic tenous stasis and thrombophlebitis."

What did he say? "You have poor circulation. A blood clot may form."

Turnabout is fair play, so let's look at a sample of jargon the psychoanalyst has been known to use.

Psychoanalyst: "I know that you believe you understand what you think I said, but I am not sure you realize that what you heard is not what I meant."

What did he say? "Hmmm."

And so it goes. The waitress refers to "moo juice" and "stacks." The plumber and the TV repairman and the garage mechanic speak a language which is alien to our tongues.

Our collective interests, which are supposed to lend themselves to attuning us to the world around us so that we can share commonalities, have instead resulted in a separatist attitude. Elitism and clannishness make us turn our heads away from one another, so that we can huddle with those we feel are really "in." We're inside our own heads, nodding solemnly to doubletalk and absorbing very little.

The dentist, electrician, etc., might just as well have said: "The frammis is connected in a spectacular globis to the stream of the terrazis. That's why the whatsis is straining to allow for cranial refractions."

There are comedians who make a living speaking in doubletalk. It's very funny, and we all laugh. Maybe we identify and feel a kinship to doubletalk as a form of humor because we hear it all around us in our daily lives.

Another form of non-intimate communication in our society can be seen in our humor. The kinship between humor and hostility has long been known. Essentially, it gives us an opportunity to speak about forbidden and even taboo areas which normally frighten us in the context of a socially acceptable setting. These areas which make us uncomfortable and which we find difficult to speak about unless we translate our feelings about them into something humorous are:

-Ethnic Jokes
-Mental Illness Jokes (The Psychiatrist Jokes)
-Death Jokes
-Mother-in-Law Jokes (and threats-to-marriage jokes)
-Sexual Problems Jokes

I. Ethnic Jokes: Here we can release our feelings about ethnic groups without having to admit either our anger or our fears.

The Polish Joke: "How do Poles form a firing squad?" "They form a circle."

"How do Poles change a light bulb?" "One man stands on a stool, holding the bulb, and two others turn him around and around."

Black Jokes: Two Blacks get on a bus in the deep south.

"All blacks in the back," says the bus driver. The two men go to the back of the bus. At the next stop, a black gets on.

"All blacks in the rear of the bus," says the driver.

"Did you hear that?" say the two young blacks sitting in the back. "Next time we'll say we are lawyers and sit up front."

"We'd better talk like lawyers," says one to the other.

Loudly, one says to the other: "I hear you are representing a rape case."

"That's right," says the other.

"Mmm, who are you representing the fucker or the fuckee?"

Jewish Jokes: Sometimes ethnic lines are crossed so that two minority groups are "covered" at the same time:

"What does Sammy Davis Jr., (a black man who has converted to Judaism) say when he looks at himself in the mirror each morning?"

"I don't know whether to be shiftless and lazy or shrewd and conniving today."

Or, the crossing of ethnic lines can be seen in:

"What's black and blue and floats in the river?"

"A Jew who tells Italian Jokes."

Italian Jokes: The Pope is addressing 250,000 Italians. He says "We never won a war, but we will have one of the first astronauts. I'll send a feather floating down, and the first one it touches will be our astronaut."

He returns to his room from the balcony, and smells a powerful aroma of garlic. Confused, he goes back out to the balcony to see 250,000 Italians blowing upwards desperately trying to stop the feather from landing.

Or, did you hear about the Italian who made himself an offer he couldn't remember?

Mixtures: Who are the three most dangerous men?

A black man with a knife, a Jew with a lawyer, and a Greek wearing sneakers.

We appear to fear the psychiatrist, and, of course, he falls into a grouping all his own:

II. Psychiatrist Jokes:

Man is on the couch. Doctor asks him what he does for a living. "I'm a psychiatrist," he says. "Then why are you coming to me?" he is asked.

"Because I can't afford my fees."

Or: A lady comes in complaining of anxiety and headaches.

Without a word, the doctor undresses her, puts her on the couch and has intercourse with her. "That took care of *my* problem, the doctor says." Now, let's take a look at *yours*."

And, of course the old classic:

Two psychiatrists pass each other in the street. One says "hello." They walk on, and the other psychiatrist says: "I wonder what he meant by that?"

III. Death: Death is something we all fear. The friendly undertaker jokes have been with us for decades. A variation on the death joke which is veiled by coupling it with another major social ill, alcoholism, is revealed in the following:

The town drunk is going to be taught a lesson. One day, out cold, he is brought to the undertaker's, placed in a coffin, and "laid to rest" with candles on the sides of the coffin, soft organ music, etc. Perhaps, the townspeople reason this may *scare* him into sobriety. The drunk awakens, finds himself on the bier, looks around and says:

"If I'm alive, what am I doing here? And, if I'm dead, why do I have to pee so badly?"

IV. Mother-In-Law: The sweet little girl became someone's sweetheart, the recipient of loving Mother's Day cards and then finds herself the dreaded mother-in-law. As the "cause" of so many marital mishaps, she finds herself added to the feared list with jokes abounding about her:

"I went for a pleasure trip with my mother-in-law—I drove her to the airport."

Or: "What's a definition of mixed emotions?"
"Watching your mother-in-law go over a cliff in your brand new Cadillac."

V. Sexual Problems: Problems of frigidity, impotence, and sexual disappointment would, quite naturally, fall into the category of the "taboo" which we make jokes about:

A woman had a cold and unresponsive husband. One day she sees an Indian Snake charmer. Watching the snake respond to the music and slowly rise, she buys a flute and hurries home to her husband, hoping it will have the same "rising" effect on her husband. He is in bed sleeping when she comes in. She plays the flute, and the blanket slowly rises. Excited, she strips, keeps playing the flute, and now, nude, takes the blanket away to find—the string on his pajamas has slowly risen and is now standing erect.

A woman buys a magic mirror:
"Mirror, mirror, make my breasts larger," she says. Her breasts grow enormous. Her boyfriend, watching, says, "Mirror, mirror, make my penis touch the ground." Immediately, his feet shrink to his knees.

The dragon is the symbol of fertility in China.
The Emperor's three daughters are asked what kind of man they want to marry.

1st daughter: "A man with a dragon on his chest."

2nd daughter: "A man with a dragon on his back."

3rd daughter: "A man with his draggin' on the floor."

Oncoming impotence in old age is a frequent fear.

Thus, we have: Three weeks after having sex with a young woman, an 85-year-old man calls the doctor to complain of a discharge from his penis.

"Do you know the woman?" the doctor asks. "Yes," says the old man. "Do you know her address, can you reach her anytime?" says the doctor. "Sure," says the old man. "Then hurry over there," says the doctor, "you're coming."

Masturbation, the classic taboo, comes in for its share of jokes:

A little boy is masturbating on the church steps. The Priest, shocked, says: "Don't you know that you can go blind from that?"
The boy looks up, continues masturbating and asks: "Father, can I just keep doing it until I need glasses?"

Or: A couple in the movies: The girl turns to the escort and whispers, "John, the man next to me is masturbating." "Ignore him," says John. She keeps telling John the man is masturbating, and John keeps telling her to ignore him. She tells John once more, and in exasperation, John says "Why can't you ignore him?"' In a plaintive voice the girl says: "How can I? He's using my hand!"

Crossing lines again, the boy is brought

to the psychiatrist, and the complaint is that the boy masturbates. "Wait in the waiting room," says the doctor. When the doctor comes out, the room is a shambles, with the boy having totally wrecked the furniture and fixtures.

"Who did that?" asks the doctor.

"I did." says the boy.

"Why did you do it?" says the doctor.

"I don't know," says the boy.

"You don't know?" asks the doctor.

"No. I was bored." says the boy.

"So why didn't you masturbate instead?" says the furious doctor.

Another type of non-intimate person often attempts to communicate too much without communicating anything. Such people can be easily distinguished. Their philosophy is shown in empty phrases like "right on," or "out of sight." Such people are too often terribly afraid of their humanity, and have found a substitute for it. They often espouse the idea that time is passing and they have to move fast to get it all in by means of substitutes for intimacy. They haven't learned that it isn't time that is passing, but *they* who are passing through time non-stop. Quickie phrases seem to answer their questions only as long as there are others to articulate them and to agree with them. When they are alone these people suffer much more than we know. They suffer from a kind of rootlessness. In their search for a reliable identity they define and overdefine themselves with as little effort and exposure—thus the least danger to themselves—as possible.

There are a number of very light to very deep levels of communication. Unless we understand that—and how we employ them—we can never understand intimacy and coping on any level.

The None-to-None Level:

How are you?

Terrible. I went bankrupt yesterday.

That's nice. How's the family?

Bad. My wife died you know.

Mm. Hmmm. Well, do give her my regards.

And how are you doing?

I'm running away.

Where to?

Any place. I'll never be back. I've had it.

Mm. Hmm. Well, have a nice trip.

Yeah. Well, so long.

So long. Great talking to you again.

There was no sharing of the person at all in this exchange. Each remained safely within the isolation of his pretense, sham, and sophistication. This is communication where nobody dares to disturb the sounds of silence.

The Allowing-a-Peek Level:
　Did you hear about Sam?
　Yes. Isn't that something?
　Who would have expected it of him?
　Yeah. And he's 47!
　I understand she's only 20.
　I hope he can get it up.
　Oh, I hear he's got a constant erection.
　Mmm. Well, gotta go.
　It's always nice speaking to you.
　Caught between Scylla and Charibdis, such people take only an occasional deep breath of the world around them. Theirs is a prison of solitary confinement. At this level we give nothing of ourselves and invite nothing of others in return.

The I'll-Show-You-My-Bellybutton Level:
　I have always like the Blacks.
　I hate niggers.
　Oh? You do?
　Yep. Don't trust them.
　I know what you mean. They're dangerous.
　Never know when they'll mug you.
　Never thought of that.
　You better think of that.
　Yeah. Like next time I'm on a dark street.
　(*Both laughing, they say good-bye.*)

　This is a step out of solitary confinement.

It's "I'll tell you some of my ideas. I'll take a chance. If you don't respond, I'll chuck it and try to please you instead. Or change the subject."

The I'll-Take-a-Chance-and-Share Level:
   I'm scared.
   Me too.
   I can't get a job.
   Me too. I think I'm too sensitive.
   That why you got fired?
   I think so.
   My problem is taking orders.
   That can be a big one.
   I get too defensive and blow up.
   Yeah. I know the feeling.
   I keep making a jackass of myself.
   We're both scared I guess.
   Yeah. But it felt good talking about it.

Someone once said that dull people talk about people, that average people speak of things and that intelligent people share feelings and ideas. At the last level the feelings underneath the words are allowed to emerge. At the true intimacy level of communicating, judgments are discarded, emotions are accepted as neither good nor bad, and the premise is that either we speak out our feelings or we will act them out.

Thus, our society today is divisive rather than intimate. Non-intimacy is expressed in the form of the expletive, the insult language, the obscene word, the professional jargon, and the inadequate communication level. Hidden in veiled hostility we can see it in our humor where even our jokes essentially are often simply stopgap measures to help us cope with what we find to be the upsetting and even frightening elements in our society.

So many ways to throw people off balance because they may be coming too close! So many techniques to create static in our communication sets! To communicate, there has to be a speaker... there has to be a listener. Sometimes, it looks as though we have stopped speaking. As though, in the ultimate, nobody is listening. But don't you believe it. We *are* sending out messages; we *are* being received on their sets.

If only those messages were sent out filled with acceptance rather than rebuff, with devotion rather than with derision! If only the extended arm had fingers outstretched in a welcoming handshake, rather than clenched into an angry fist. If only we could face one another with trust, instead of responding to messages which fill us with fear of one another.

Too many of us are so alienated and separated by our conditioning that we seem incapable of functioning as whole persons; we seem incapable of achieving intimacy.

We have learned all the differences, few of the similarities. We live off what we have been exposed to—a society which breeds distrust and hostility. We forget that "all those people out there" have needs and desires and emotions and fears and hang-ups and miseries very much like our own. We have become incapable of effective communication, and are emotionally at war with those around us. We are not aware of sights and sounds, not aware of our own innards. We forget that a bounteous world can supply us with all we need.

We can't be ourselves because we've never learned how; we cannot reveal ourselves because we're afraid we'll be unloved or disliked or despised or thought stupid. And yet, unthinkingly, we permit ourselves to be triggered, by virtually any life situation or problem, to immature, destructive responses. This obviously isn't a very efficient way of getting close to people.

Almost invariably we look outside ourselves for the cause of our problems as well as their solutions—the world owes us a living, and it had damn well better provide it. Our desires become addictions. Any challenge to our particular "gotta-have-it" pattern sets off a low-level reaction like that of a frightened or frustrated child.

The Collector, the Manipulator, and the Brat

Look, look, look.
I am a robot.

See me walk.
One foot up.
One foot down.

Chug, chug, chug.
See my arms wave.
As my feet move.

I'll tell you how I got.
To be a robot.
If you tell me how you got.
To be a robot.

That's only fair.
Isn't it?

Chapter 2

The Collector, The Manipulator and The Brat

The non-intimate society we have been looking at has seen the emergence of three distinct types. Did society produce the types or vice versa? It's a moot point at the moment. But an awareness of the existence of the three types is fundamental in any study of intimacy.

These three types are:

>   The Collector
>   The Manipulator
>   The Brat

The behavior of these three are characterized by instinctual, no-choice patterns. As their names suggest, that behavior is exhibited in the drive to collect, the urge to manipulate and the desire for uninterrupted pleasure.

The Collector, the Manipulator, and the Brat are in all of us. The degree to which they reside there dictates the extent of non-intimacy we exhibit. Sometimes one is uppermost; sometimes all three jockey for position.

I will not go into a sociological study of how the home, the family and the school helped to program the unintimate Collector, Manipulator and Brat. Such a study would be beyond the scope of this book. There are a plethora of books which go into great detail, espousing a wide variety of theories on how the faulty programming of children produces problems within our society. What is of fundamental importance here is that it was quite inevitable that a grabbing, competitive, snarling society such as we have been describing should have spawned the Collector, the Manipulator, and the Brat. Like the Phoenix, they raised themselves out of the ashes of whatever intimacy could have or did exist at one time. We want to recognize them—it's *terribly* important to recognize them, so that when we see them around us we will know how the alienated— the Collector, the Manipulator, and the Brat—sow their seeds of separatism. Most important of all, when we see them in *ourselves*—which is truly the goal of this book—we will recognize them for what they are: The destructive enemies from our conditioned, programmed past who produce pain and suffering to those around us, and, of course, to ourselves.

The three figures from our earliest programming all whisper repeatedly "I could be happy if..." and what they need to finish that sentence dictates their behavior.

The Collector:

The Collector whispers into the ear of the addicted and non-intimate man: "I could be happy if I felt secure." The Collector believes that more is better, that something different and newly acquired is better. This belief is attached to his security. It could be money, or houses, wives, lovers, husbands, cars, trophies, diplomas, the next one, the next one, and the next one. Some collectors collect the steps on the Stairway to Success. Essentially, the Collector sees security in a stockpile fashion, and he is at battle with the world to "get his."

The poor Collector! What he has never learned is that security can't come from outside oneself, but from the inside. As with all unintimate people, the Collector's world is made up of "others" who are seen as objects. They are in the world as friend or foe depending on whether they help him feel secure or threaten that security.

The Collector has always had trouble with himself—with the acceptance of himself. He sees constant imagined threats to that self. What was lacking in his early programming was pride and dignity in himself. Dignity is an essential component of identity; and identity, if we look within ourselves is essential to happiness.

We are doomed to frustrations from birth. All we can hope to do is handle them as they arise. The child who very early learns that "bad" situations are someone else's fault very quickly learns to try to outwit the slings and arrows of life's outrageous fortunes. Frustrations are not to be avoided and denied; they are to be seen as parts of life which have to be clarified, evaluated and then handled.

The Collector learns early in life to bluff, rationalize, lie, play it cool, never expose legitimate curiosity or spontaneous feelings. He is so concerned with his sense of security, with trying to be "with it" at all times, that he is ever at the ready and prepared to fight any person or situation wherein he may be the figure of scorn or contempt. His need for security directs him towards seeing people in terms of objects, and he learns to equate people and things equally.

The Manipulator:

If the Collector wanted more security, the Manipulator hears sweet words of never-ending power whispered into his ear. The words say: "I could be happy if I could manipulate and control people and things around me." The manipulator is programmed to need power for his happiness. What interferes with that power, or threatens to interfere with it, produces his explosive behavior and his non-intimate reactions. The Manipulator hasn't learned that we all have all the power we need. He still remembers the early years when he was weak, inadequate, inferior, and surrounded by a world of giants. He is still compensating for the power deficiencies which he felt as a child.

Life becomes a constant power struggle for the Manipulator. His message to the world-at-large: "I need power to control the people and manipulate the things in my life for me to be happy." Or, "I need to be sure nobody has that power over me. If you go along with it we can avoid a power struggle. Otherwise, I'll see you as a threat to my happiness."

The Manipulator—like all unintimate people—wears a mask wherever he or she goes. Such masks hold within them, unseen, the thwarted expressions of their feelings. The Manipulator won't tolerate defeat and uses the masks—including his own—as a way of warding off defeat. If he fears being laughed at or scorned, he wears a mask which will, hopefully, push away those who would exploit him or use him. He'll have the edge, for he will move in fast, assert himself to establish his position and his rights, and then in typically unintimate fashion, move away again. Oh yes, he would like to drop the mask, for he is human. But he can't. He won't take a chance, for his fears and tensions which equate power with survival keep the mask on the bridge of his nose, and he goes about gasping for air.

The Manipulator, the power struggler, is never thankful for or accepting of the fact that he has influence over other people. He is totally convinced that when he denies his authority, his power, his strength, he affirms his uselessness. As a result he is equally convinced that others will see no value in paying attention to him. That prospect is so frightening, that he constantly protects himself against such a contingency and steamrolls his way, like a bulldozer, through life.

The Brat:

The words the Brat uses are: "I could be happy if the world provided me with all the pleasures I feel I have to have..."

Usually those pleasures relate to sex, the Ultimate Sensation, the Road to Orgasm. He tries to find happiness by providing himself with more and better pleasurable sensations and activities. It doesn't have to be sex, however. It could also be food, music, sports, a soap opera, drinking—anything which serves to offer pleasure. The Brat is pleasure-oriented and is furious when the outside world doesn't cooperate with his or her games or threatens to cut them short. Ultimately, to the pleasure-seeker, life is a series of competitive moves and countermoves. He is constantly trying to rearrange the world to conform to an earlier model which provided easy access to his or her needs for the fun time, the feast time, the game time. The Freudian would see the pleasure seeker as the oral personality who sucks on the nipple of the world with gusto and cries with rage when the nipple is taken away or appears to run dry.

As with all non-intimate behavior, all that can be hoped for are flashes of pleasure which can't be sustained.

The family which programs the child into the Brat produces the ultimate pleasure-seeker. Such a family usually deteriorates into a state of war. At that point, of course, all teaching is blocked. Such a state calls for going easy on "blocking" techniques which might "frustrate" the child. Such a family tries to avoid outright prohibitions and "no's", and goes heavily into "substitute" techniques so that possibilities always exist for some substitute gratification even when the immediate gratification can't be achieved.

The problem: As a child, the Brat remained on the tension-discharge level longer than he needed to. His tantrums and demands were tolerated way past the time a child can be expected to have the means for control. The Brat emerges from such a setting remaining on a primitive discharge level if for no other reason than nothing more has ever been required of him or her! When the expectations of a child are not increased, challenges are reduced and finally eliminated—along with any self-esteem which accompanies successful handling of challenges.

The Brat has learned to gratify his impulses without delay. Growing up, for him, did not allow for much time spent on learning to forego some kind of immediate gratification in order to acquire some more of it in the long run. Life usually requires that we learn to delay our first or second impulses somewhere along the line. The Brat wants quick and direct solutions rather than complex ones. That's his problem, and his problem in time becomes a problem to all of us.

Let's face it: Who *really* wants to tolerate, to postpone pleasures? But if we are not to collide with each other constantly, we must develop frustration tolerance and give some space to the other fellow so as not to crowd him.

The parent who ignores, neglects, overindulges through guilt, and pampers as a way of "shutting him up" produces what is essentially a forgotten child. Such a child—later the Brat—may learn to seek nonhuman activities and equate all types of pleasure with being loved. He may find himself unable to come close to children and later to adults, because he is unable to love. He becomes the movie addict, the TV addict, the bookworm, the alcoholic, the drug addict, the addicted golfer, and so on. In time he may become the ultimate buyer of affection and belongingness like his counterpart, the Collector. These deaden his need for intimacy.

The need for communication, intimacy, and passion lessen more and more, and the pleasure-loving side of him grows. At that point meaningful love does not come easily to him. The resistance of the world in providing constant and ever-ready gratification coupled with his addictive need for unconditional gratification create pressures which make the Brat turn to the search for substitute satisfactions.

When the Collector, the Manipulator, and the Brat within us find that the World has not supplied them with what they feel they need to meet their addictions, they experience a wide variety of unintimate sensations and emotions.

The Collector worries that someone may steal his source of fulfillment—his money, his girl, her fur coat, or whatever he or she collects for security.

"It's mine—you can't have it," underlies what is shown to the world as jealousy—the Collector-type of jealousy.

When "I need more," is coupled with "get out of my way or I'll run you over," the combination produces the anger typical of the Manipulator and the Collector.

Cynical thinking and behaving is typical of the Collector, the Manipulator, and the Brat who can easily lament that they don't "get enough," or that "everyone gets more." Ultimately, they see the world as a lousy world, and everything is "unfair."

The suspicion of the Collector, the Manipulator, and the Brat make them see threats all about them. "I'll have to watch you, or you'll take what I have or what I need," says the Collector. "You're not going to push me around, and don't you forget it," says the Manipulator. "If I don't keep my eye on you, you'll take away my pleasure, and I won't have any fun," says the Brat.

The penalty of most unintimate behavior—loneliness, isolation and boredom—sees the Manipulator, the Collector, and the Brat lamenting that they don't get "any fun out of life," with a constant whining that "I just have no luck," and "You have to watch everybody because they are out to get what they can from you."

Even when things are going fine, the Manipulator and the Collector and the Brat worry that the source of supply will dry up.

The Manipulator makes his characteristic rapier thrust at the world before it can happen; the Collector worries that while things are going well now, it "may not last; maybe the supply will run out," (and he wants 20 of them while he can get them). The Brat is just generally miserable unless the supply is steady, flowing and unlimited, for *any* interference with his pleasures is a condition not to be tolerated.

And all three remain worried and tense and anxious in the midst of plenty or in the expectation that somewhere around the corner a famine must surely be waiting.

And so it goes. The Manipulator overreacts and keeps pushing his way about whenever he feels a threat; the Collector has apprehension that he hasn't collected enough yet; the Brat just explodes into temper tantrums even in the midst of plenty if he feels that something or someone may stop his moments of pleasure.

It must be so terribly exhausting to expend so much psychic energy, and to experience so much anger and conflicting emotions because we aren't getting enough of what we need to feel secure, strong and satisfied.

A loving relation between a man and a woman calls for compassion, intimacy, and communication as well as passion. It's composed also of liking, abandon, and respect. The unintimate so often finds it hard to trust completely. There is no one with whom he can be completely open, no one who by his or her presence provokes our spontaneous delight, and no one in whose presence he or she can abandon all controls and all defenses in an unguarded passion of intimacy.

Since the Manipulator, the Collector, and the Brat embody all the elements of true unintimacy, and since the Manipulator controls, the Collector continues to acquire more and more, and the Brat seeks greater and greater forms of uninterrupted pleasure, it would seem to be only natural that they are all within the person we call *The Unintimate One*.

To understand intimacy, we have to have a clearer picture of this paradox we call Man; an awareness of how his mind betrays him and sacrifices him to a set of beliefs which easily can destroy him. What has to *happen* before we can become intimate?

The "I" in Intimacy

Am I intimate now?
I don't know.

I don't *feel* differently.
So what have I gained
By all this?

Maybe only one thing.
What you had lost.

Lost? What had I lost?

You.

The most important ingredient in the formula for intimacy comes down to one word: acceptance. True, honest, real acceptance of myself and of you. Acceptance, to the intimate person, does not mean placating, or being condescending; it is not simply tolerating or compromising or resigning himself or herself to a situation. To the intimate person, acceptance includes taking responsibility for one's actions, acknowledging another's point of view, living in the here and now. It's being aware of the *now*, not pigeonholing other people into old and stale notions. Above all, it is experiencing what is happening inside the gut, and feeling free to communicate this to others.

Acceptance creates a safe place for the other person. Finally, acceptance removes the dreaded burden of having to be right, or the deadening fear of being wrong. In a sense, such acceptance allows a person to take full responsibility for what is happening when his or her life just isn't working.

Our entire lives can be measured by making an analogy between life and the familiar twelve-inch ruler. The first eleven inches of life are made up of "getting there," or "arriving" or "winning." Those eleven inches include "being right," and "making it." Happiness is then measured by care, money, Climbing the Stairs to Success, or becoming Mother of the Year. Trophies are collected which are called Titles, Diplomas, Promotions, and Position in Life. That was supposed to spell happiness, but for too many in this unintimate world the moment comes when the Big House, and the New Car and all the other *stuff* does not do the trick. Is it possible that all that collecting and achieving does not bring happiness, warmth, contentment and the quality existence it promised? Were we conned? The gnawing question emerges: if all that doesn't work, doesn't create a sense of aliveness and make us happy, what in hell will?

It is at this crucial point that we begin to search for and recognize our need for that last inch—the inch which will give quality to our lives. *Quality*, not quantity. Only in the knowledge we can acquire in that last inch lies a chance to experience true happiness. Happiness is not something you buy, something the world gives you in a pretty, packaged gift. Happiness is not something you GET. Happiness is something you ARE. You are because you create what you are. You are the creator of your life and you finally have to take responsibility for the way it is; have to give up proving you are right. The issue is not—never was—a question of wrong or right. Only when you accept that the way it is, *is*, can you steer your own ship and begin to create your world, your reality.

The intimate person accepts his addictions. He accepts that we all have the Collector, the Manipulator and the Brat in him. He also accepts that he is responsible for everything that happens to him and is not fixed on a position of having to be right. He pauses when he is emotionally triggered, when his button is pressed. He looks at what is happening inside him, and experiences that. He can identify when the voice of the Collector, the Manipulator and the Brat are whispering in his ear. He identifies the button which is being pressed and which sets him off. And then he selects his course of action based on choice and preference. When the intimate person makes a choice at that point, he finds that the options are limitless. Creating a reality which moves into intimacy is never again having to be limited to robot-like decisions based on mindless emotional binges.

Experiments with rats have shown an interesting phenomenon. If a rat is put into a cage with three tunnels, and there is a piece of cheese at the end of just one tunnel, the rat sniffs around until he finds the cheese and he goes down that tunnel. Forever after he will, on repeated trials, go down the tunnel with the cheese in it. But if the cheese is placed in another tunnel, the rat may go down the first tunnel and be surprised to find no cheese there any more. He may continue to do that two or three more times. But soon enough he will stop going down the empty tunnel and begin sniffing at the others. When he finds that the cheese has been placed in *another* tunnel he will go down that one. One way or another he will always find the tunnel with the cheese in it, no matter how much sniffing it takes.

But humans don't do that. They keep going down the tunnel without any cheese in it forever. Why? Like the rat, Man may have once thought there was cheese there. Maybe at one time there was. But what makes him keep rushing down the tunnel when he *knows* there is no cheese there? It is his firm conviction that it is the right thing to do, or the hope that if the cheese was once there, if he waits long enough, he'll find cheese again. Other times he goes down the tunnel where no cheese awaits because he thinks *others* feel he should go there. And he even continues his aimless and painful searching in a tunnel without any rewards or satisfaction for him long after he understands why he does it. He becomes a robot.

When this occurs, Man has rejected choice. He is not aware of the limitless options open to him. No self-respecting rat would keep going down a tunnel with no cheese in it, not for *any* reason. The rat knows that the real reward—in a sense what really *matters*—is getting that cheese. He knows that the cheese will satisfy his hunger and make him happy. He is not concerned with being right or wrong, with *shoulds*, or *oughttos* or *What Will They Think?*

What about us? What about Man, who is considered the most intelligent animal on this planet? Why *can't* we have limitless choice, steering that ship, in charge of our destiny, at cause and not at effect? Why do we so often have to be right? Why are we so afraid of being wrong, being called wrong, or being "found out?"

The unintimate is riddled with beliefs that he considers sacred, sacrosanct, and inviolable. He really believes that *more is better* and he will defend that point of view and others equally fruitless to the death. *Literally*, he will defend his point of view to the death. If you doubt that statement, if you don't think that our belief systems or points of view which are recorded on our tapes in those computers we call our minds can and will destroy us and our very being just consider these examples:

A man runs into a burning building to recover his insurance policies. A woman runs back into that burning building to get her jewels. The child runs back to get his whatsis.

A teenager swerves his shiny car to avoid a dent and runs the risk of going over a cliff.

A man who has just been robbed of ten dollars chases the armed burglar.

They were all defending a point of view, a strong belief. They were quite ready when their tapes told them to sacrifice their beings. The greatest sacrifice of all: winding up dead.

Just consider. If a point of view is *that* important, literally to be defended to the death, the intimate person is wise enough to accept other people's points of view as quite literally connected with their very survival. He accepts as a truth that being wrong or right and the fear of admitting that is so important to people that intimacy is impossible unless that rightness door is first closed. He recognizes it in himself; he always works on it and tries to accept total responsibility at all times. He recognizes it in others; he acknowledges the genuineness of their feelings about being right and knows people have to get over that immensely important hurdle before they can even begin to work on intimacy problems.

By acknowledging the other you get agreement. When you say "I understand that," or "I see your point of view," people know where you are and they are still not wrong. Don't ponder on *why* not being wrong is so powerfully, incredibly important to people. It just is. Accept that. Even if you don't agree with them, you can still acknowledge their point of view. Only then are they ready to listen to your problem and take a look at *your* point of view. When you close the rightness door for the other person he can finally deal with the issue or the problem or the relationship, because he feels he is going to *survive*. (*What? Is this guy telling me that the other person's idea, notions, points of view and beliefs are so powerful, so demanding of acceptance by others that if he thinks you feel he is wrong he thinks he won't survive?* Yes, my friend. That's exactly what I am saying.) When you remove the threat of wrongness from his point of view, you actually acknowledge that he is okay. Agreement happens. Intimacy can begin.

Have we said you should placate, be condescending, even lie just to agree? Hardly. Lots of people want you to choose where you are going. When you do, others see where you are at. By not making him wrong, by acknowledging the genuineness of his feelings and his position, you have not cancelled his vote and invalidated him. *The last inch is being at truth with yourself.* Knowing what's so for you. Looking at it, watching the river go by and just leaving it alone. You can't change it.

The intimate person knows that time is an illusion, and that it is only an interval between two points. The past is measured by what happened *then*—an hour, a day, a month, a year ago. The future is measured by what *will* happen—an hour, a day, a month, a year from now. But at the split-second instant of its happening, before any time interval can be built up, there is this second, this *now*. The experience itself. And the intimate person is most comfortable in the now, not fixated on the guilt and anger of the past or the apprehension and anxiety of the future. The *now* is the safe space for the intimate person, unlike the unintimate who swings pendulum-style back and forth between the past and the future.

It's all *now*. Here and now. Life is just successive moments of events of *now*. You are constantly clicking off those moments of *now*. A choice—any choice—is an idea. A notion. You choose it. Most importantly, you can choose to construct only those ideas which will serve *your* purpose—and you do it consciously. At that moment, what you have chosen from the limitless options, you bring to your reality. The point is that reality is ours. We created it. We gave it significance and decided to make it very important. Before we did that it never had any significance. We elected to put the significance into the reality of the dirty word, the ethnic attitude, the belief we cling to. But what is, after all, *is*. Don't resist it. Get clear on your ideas of what you *really* experience, then choose what you want to do. When you acknowledge that, come to agreement with yourself, communicate it and experience it out. You now have a reality you can accept or a new reality which you just created.

Start small. Let's say you want to go shopping. Or you just want to open the door. Ever think that doors are concepts and that we created the reality attached to them? How would you ever get out of a room if you came from a planet where there were no doors and the symbolism of the door was alien to you? But anyway, you want to open the door. You choose to do that and at that second you have agreement with you. At that point, you have created reality, and the door is already open. You can have what you choose, because only time and space separate you from getting up and opening that door. If it is truly your intention to open it, you may be temporarily derailed by the phone ringing, or having to turn the TV off. But you *will* open that door!

If your intention is not an act, but the communicating of feelings, you can create that reality too. The intimate person has no difficulty communicating his feelings. He keeps in touch with them in the *now*, constantly practicing how to know what he is experiencing and communicating that experience. That's what we mean by experiencing it out. If he is sad, angry, unhappy, bored or whatever, he does not avoid it, look away, deny it. He moves into it, cleans up what he wants to clean up, and gets over the frustration. And, in the most remarkable way, once he has communicated it, experienced it fully, experienced it out, the pain, agony and frustration just goes and the person feels better. He is at truth with what is so for him. (What more could a person ask of himself?) Isn't that what steering a ship is all about?

To admit being bored when you are bored

can be satisfying. Don't deny you are bored. Find what is so for you, what is true for you. When it hurts, hurt with it. When it's terrific, let it be terrific. Tell yourself you are happy when you are unhappy and you will only remain unhappy that much longer. Try to laugh when you are sad, and you not only remain sad, you are out of touch with the real *you*, the *you* which you are truly experiencing. If it's a sad movie, or a sad story in life, it's appropriate to be sad at that movie and not sit laughing in the middle of a group which is accepting being sad. You can't change it. Just let it be exactly the way it is. At that moment you are not addicted to old programming which keeps you chug-chugging away like a robot.

People who sponsor and encourage intimacy help you to accept and tolerate you. They do it by opening themselves up and revealing themselves to you. I truly feel that I can only know that much of myself which I have had the courage to confide to you. Such intimacy is intimacy on a dimension which calls for acceptance, responsibility, and a willingness to admit honest feelings to yourself and others. We aren't speaking of some old-hat positive thinking program here. This is not *positive* thinking. It is *honest* thinking. Honest thinking works, simply because it is satisfying.

We have spoken about creating a safe space for another person as an essential for intimacy. You don't want to be crowded and pressed; the other fellow wants and deserves the same space so that he does not feel threatened. Think of it as a body-bubble which we wrap around ourselves. The bubble is transparent so that the person can be seen, but there is a huge zipper which has to be unzipped by the person. You can probe the bubble, make indentations in it. But unless the person opens the zipper there is no way you can get in. In the crowded earth's geography, the body-bubble is ours, our very own.

Some bubbles are much wider in dimension than others, depending on what the individual will allow. But everybody has one. Fear keeps the body-bubble closed. Fear of being made to look foolish; being made to look wrong. Or a biggie-fear of making a mistake and being rejected. If we move in too fast, others will move back, protecting the body-bubble from the invasion. Even staring at a person too long can be perceived as an attempt at puncturing the bubble. If someone tries too hard at first contact, looks too long, moves in too close, we sense it, feel annoyed and are on guard. We feel the other person pushed inside the body-bubble before he was invited in. We feel we do not have a safe space.

We can create that safe space for the other person by not making him wrong, and by accepting responsibility for any interpersonal problems which may arise. He needs a chance to expand his own space. After all, if people had not gotten in the way we would all have gone where our space expansion was taking us when we were infants. But THEY said you shouldn't, you have to, you gotta, you should, you can't do this, you must do that, and what will others think. Soon enough the Custom Tailor came into our lives and measured us for our body-bubble, letting us know we needed one to survive. And they derailed us, when we couldn't expand our own space and couldn't provide a safe space for others any longer.

You really *believed* all those things. You stopped simply *being*, just a host for the myriad experiences you were enjoying by just being. And you stopped trusting in your experiences in the here and now, and built up a belief system which you trusted instead.

> Fuck
> Jew
> Nigger
> Democrat

The words became significant only when *you* made them so. They never were significant until *you* did that. Until *you* got a point of view about them. *You* put the importance and the venom and, yes, the significance into those words and notions. When you can introduce a little more "so what" into your point of view, you have a reasonable stab at being intimate and not just a chug-chugging robot. Remember, once you decided to open the door, you couldn't—if it were truly your intention—be derailed. Unless you chose another option. The only things you can ever do in life are those things you expand your space to include. What derails you? The point of view you take, the notions you adopt, the ego which develops from that, and then your decision to defend that notion to the death. That's not a surprising idea. Unintimate people all around us are terribly busy making things terribly important and significant and then defending their notions to the death. Most non-intimate people are pretty dead anyway, because they are not aware, not awake.

Being *awake* comes from putting yourself out there for others to know, to see, to experience and to observe. Doing it without concern about being right or being wrong. Being *aware* is recognizing how all those beliefs manipulate you and lead your life, and keep you at the effect of those beliefs rather than at cause when you steer your own ship. Take away all those beliefs, and what have you got? Just you. Your Self.

The unintimates of the world don't dare question those beliefs and see their experiences as the only truth. That's why the unintimates of the world have a basic sameness: they are all fighting for what they consider their very survival. To them survival is the Name of the Game. Such people create different points of view about what constitutes the best "survival" tactics and spend their lives defending them. Such people consider themselves "realistic," for to them that truly is reality.

But what *is* reality? It is just agreements. We agree to a door, a chair, a table, and they exist in what we call our reality. In the same way we agree about our stupid neighbor, the Blacks, the Jews, the girl with blonde hair, the teen-ager with jeans. We agree all over the place to concepts we don't even experience. You can't *experience* a concept. A concept is only a *symbol* of the experience. There is a huge difference between the symbols of experience and the experience itself. You can't disagree with a concept and hope it will be different. People who never learned the secrets of intimacy got ideas and notions, constructed them, agreed to them, and made it their reality. Want to move from non-intimacy to intimacy? Just recreate your reality. Acknowledge that *truth* is only what you *experience*, not what you believe, and take responsibility for that. Then try out a new notion; construct one on intimacy, not apartness and otherness, and agree to *that*. That's not easy to do, for we have pretty much agreed to preserve and pay homage to our old beliefs. But intimacy and coping, my friends, are an agreement, not a goal.

How did we get all those ideas, those concepts? The reasons don't matter. There are only results and reasons why you don't get those results. When you start searching for reasons, you are just looking for ways to justify your actions. Look for rightness and you know that wrongness is around somewhere and you have come back, full circle. That's imitating and aping and looking to be "right."

Want to imitate? Keep listening to the old tapes. Want to create and not imitate? Start choosing. I see many successful people every day. Repeatedly I hear that they never expected to be doing the work they eventually wound up doing. They just *chose*, and were responsible for those choices. They didn't "try" but kept right on choosing and *did*. They didn't dwell on reasons.

Just think. If you had to know how and why you enjoy life you'd also have to ask for a reason for everything that went on in your life. In every situation. What a mind-boggling thought! It's past. Leave it alone. When you play and replay pictures of the past, you're asking for the sameness and exactness which the beliefs in your mind love to keep you stuck in. That way there is no change, no chance for intimacy. The mind is very consistent in hanging on to its beliefs and shooting those old pictures on your tapes back to you. It tries to be consistently right. Especially when you get into a situation which even remotely resembles an earlier one.

You see a Big Nose. A Fat Woman. A Sweaty Man. A Red Haired Girl. A Teacher. A Cop. At the instant you see them, the old pictures start flashing by.

But pause, expand your space to take them in. Just talk to yourself. You may laugh at the old robot and maybe even say "there it goes again. It just won't quit!" At that instant you've dealt a crushing blow to Old Robot. Why? Because you have had an essential shift in your sense of yourself.

The most valuable information we can get is not the date, the year, the quotation, the Capital of the State. That's just more *stuff*. More collecting. The most valuable information is what brings a shift in your essential sense of yourself. If you experience a *shift* in your sense of satisfaction with life, then the time spent is valuable.

That's the last inch. Putting it differently, the most important information in the world, *without* a shift in your essential sense of yourself, is worthless. I have asked authors and drama critics how they determine the value of a book, or a movie or a play. Invariably they reply: "By how much it affects me—puts me in touch with myself—explains a reason for my being alive." That's a paraphrase, of course, but it's a variation on the same theme. Earn more, win more, manipulate for the most important things in the world and without that effect on the Self all the information and content is just more stuff, and quite worthless in quality. It's just plodding along the trail, finding more ways to be right.

Do you want to be right? It's easy. Just say to somebody, anybody, "Don't be a jackass; stop being so stupid; dammit, you are acting like a baby." Stuff like that. Don't react to his behavior and share your experience; just go right on judging him. Make him wrong, W-R-O-N-G. Then watch him start his act. That breeze you just felt was the rightness door opening up again for him. See the red light flashing on his head? He's getting ready to defend. Now you have somebody to deal with who will do what he feels he or she has to do to be "all right," and to "survive." To pronounce himself okay and justify himself. He'll run his act through, and you'd better take responsibility for that. After all, wasn't that exactly what *you* did, run your own act through, when you called him a jackass?

Whether you are intimate or not depends, then, on knowing you have your own acts and your own addictions. What is *your* act? Is it Father? Boss? I'm-Just-A-Poor-Victim? I'm-Bright-And-I'll-Prove-It-To-You? Look, look, look, see me climb the Stairway to Success? I'm really a jackass but please don't notice? Maybe it's College Professor? Maybe it's Archie Bunkering? Do you know that some analysts have an act going for them called The Analyst?

If you want to play Father, spelled F-A-T-H-E-R, it's okay. But get *satisfaction* in your relationship with your children, husband, co-workers, or students. Or just with people. A relationship between people is not the same as Father-And-Child. Relationships between people are satisfying. The other is a game. A role. Football, golf, making money, getting rich, getting diplomas—those are games. And then they can be fun. Games are stupid, but they are fun. After all, life is a game.

But don't expect satisfaction from games. Life also includes suffering and nasty stuff. The Brat loves games but gets little satisfaction from his games. Why? Because a game is when what is *not* is better and more important that what *is*. When what *is* is more important than what is *not*, the game is over. So, a game is great, but it's not satisfying. Only gratifying. You may experience gratification from lots of games, lots of acts, but only if you are in touch with YOU can you experience satisfaction. There's room for games and making money and such because they remove the monotony of life. But knowing it's a game is when you choose it and know when to drop it because you know the truth of what you are experiencing when you experience it.

Because this is it. This is as good as it gets. No magic powder, no fairy godmother fighting the Wicked Witch of the West. If you get that this is it, get in touch with it, experience it and then communicate that, you can change the whole quality of your life. You can be satisfied, complete, whole, perfect,—and intimate—as you are. This minute. In the now. Not when you are 75.

What we need at this point is a step-by-step *formula* to help you cope with the world around you. Here it is. It's essential, for unless we can cope with frustrations there isn't even a *chance* for intimacy.

THE FORMULA

When the Collector, the Manipulator and the Brat are triggered, and their expectations and demands fail to get "enough" from the environment and the world, they make us go on emotional binges which crank up our computers, and we run our acts through. To help us cope with those addictions, there are a number of steps we should keep in mind:

1. *Don't make him or her wrong.* Avoid that by taking responsibility for whatever happens, and remembering that you only force people to defend their positions mightily when they feel they have been put in touch with their enormous sense of inferiority. That's why they have to cover their dread that in reality others may see them for what they fear they are: a little dumb and a little crazy.

2. *Tune in.* Listen to those voices inside. Be absolutely sure of one thing: the Collector, the Manipulator and the Brat are on those tapes of yours, always whining and keeping you fixed on a position of having to be right and follow the same old patterns. At least be aware when your own buttons have been pressed, and you are overreacting. How can we *not* know when we are being terribly emotional?

3. *When you start to go into your act, try to isolate the culprit.* Is it the Collector who

is whispering in your ear? The Manipulator? The Brat? A combination of all three?

4. *Once you have identified that lower level state of consciousness, commit yourself to choices.* Talk to yourself. The dialogue could run something like this: "Wow, I'm really experiencing an addiction. What am I feeling? My heart is beating fast, my stomach is in a knot, I'm starting to sweat. I'm getting a headache. I feel like exploding. (Or whatever). Is it my security which is being attacked—the Collector? Am I feeling overwhelmed, pushed around, manipulated and helpless—the Manipulator? Did something come up to interfere with my pleasure—the Brat?"

5. *Stay with it.* Keep talking to yourself. This person, thing, idea, situation has no significance and no importance unless I make it important. What am I experiencing *now?* What reality am I creating?

6. *With that question, the one that probes into the experience of the moment, you are into true reality—the awareness of the here and now.* Don't do that, refuse to take responsibility for what is going on within your Self, and you'll remain addicted, reaching more deeply into your own survival kit.

7. *Now that I know what I'm experiencing, I'll move towards a preference.* I'll go for a preference knowing full well that I

may not get my choice, that we win some and lose some. But on that lowest level, I'm just playing out my act. I know now that my act is just scene after scene of having to be right. On that lowest level, where the Manipulator, the Collector and the Brat are leading me around, there is a *gotta-gotta* quality to everything. With preferences, I can accept that they are, after all, only preferences, and I can accept not getting them; at the preference level I am no longer addicted, mindless and robotized.

8. *I guess I lost this one.* (Or, how about that? I moved towards my preference and I got this one). I experienced, felt the anger, fear, sense or manipulation or insecurity. I saw my act—the bully, the victim, the bright one, the parent, the child—whatever.

9. *Having experienced, acknowledged what I was experiencing*, accepted responsibility for that, I have communicated it, experienced it out, made a choice and moved towards it. The cheese is mine because I didn't go up the old tunnel. And the old frustrations are gone. It was a tough one, this particular situation, but I handled it.

10. *I guess traffic jams and other things which used to drive me crazy have a raison d'etre somewhere in my past.* I can look at that and watch the tape as it goes by. But I know I can't edit that tape or change it or

erase it. I can only look at it and accept it. What is, is.

At that point we can flow with the river, with the situation, with what used to throw us into addictions and keep us there. There will be other times. They never stop. But you're on top of it. You can handle it. You can at least cope. You don't have to paddle furiously upstream, sometimes even against the rapids.

Interesting. Once aware of our addictions, we can now see them as they operate in others. We can't help them, we can see them struggling and just hope to keep reprogramming ourselves. It's a never-ending process but a pleasant one once you master it. Life isn't pleasant when you don't master it, and are its slave. At that point we are experiencing what is, not staying fixed in a position which paralyzes us with guilt and anger from the past and apprehension and anxiety over the future. We can experience the truth and the reality of the moment.

Once we are at one with our world, it becomes *us*, not *me*. Us people. Us trees. You can cope, you can experience, you can communicate and you can steer from choice. And then—and *then*—you can love, for you become alive and aware when you risk being yourself in relationship to others and can finally trust the other person to accept you as you are.

Chapter 3

Intimacy in Action

Now it is time to look at intimacy in action, in typical life situations which we all face and run into constantly. This section will be broken down into the following:
- An Essential Principle for True Intimacy
- Problems in Life Which Frustrate Us
- How the Unintimate Person Would React
- How the Intimate Person Would React

I. AN ESSENTIAL PRINCIPLE FOR TRUE INTIMACY:

Knowing your addictions. Recognizing that The Collector, Manipulator and Brat won't quit working on you.

*A Typical Problem in Life
which Frustrates Us:*

I feel my boss is manipulating me, pushing me around. I feel underpaid and used. I never felt he realized my value to the company.

The Unintimate Reaction:

I'm not going to take this crap any longer. I'm sick and tired of being pushed around. People have done this to me as long as I can remember. I know I'm right—anyone would agree with me. I have plenty of reasons for feeling this way. One of these days I'll tell him off and then quit this damned job. I just haven't any money put away yet. Much as I hate this job and the boss, I can't take a chance with all my expenses. I don't know what he wants. I work hard, and am good at my job. That bastard just isn't reasonable. There he goes, looking at me like that again. I know what that means. He's fed up with me.

The Intimate Reaction:

This job isn't giving me the satisfactions I need. I take responsibility for that. I'm just going to have to make a choice and quit or stay. It's not a question of who is wrong or right, because my boss has his point of view too. After all, it's a business, and he isn't running it just to take care of my needs.

When I feel pushed around and not appreciated, and that old Manipulator and Collector tell me I need more and more to feel secure, I'm not going to go into my act and start the old robot going. That'll get me nowhere.

He just gave me one of those looks. What do I experience when he looks at me? My tapes say "he's fed up with you; you've had it; he hates you." But he's not my daddy, or teacher. I guess I have to look at those tapes and what's there about bosses. I can't do much about the tapes, but I can look at them and I can accept them.

What does it mean when he looks at me? If I let go of those old tapes and those old beliefs it just means he is looking at me. That's all that's happening. There! I looked back and smiled and son-of-a-gun he smiled back. I just acknowledged him, didn't make him wrong, and he doesn't have to defend any point of view. He's coming over. I'm going to communicate what I'm experiencing to him.

You: Hi, Boss. Saw you looking at me and I said to myself: "Oh, oh, wonder what I did." (*Laughs*)

Boss: (*Laughing*) I know. A lot of people feel that way. Used to feel that way myself. I was wondering if you'd seen that ball peen hammer anywhere. Can't find the damned thing.

You: Nope. But I'll give it to you if I find it. Things are always missing around here. Sometimes I think that if my head wasn't connected to my shoulders...

Boss: (*Nodding*) Yeah, I know. (*Boss starts to leave*).

You: Oh, by the way, can I speak with you for a few minutes later?

Boss: Sure. Come in at four.

You: Great. (*Boss leaves*)
Well, I guess I'll talk to him about a raise. That's my choice. My preference. Maybe I'll get it, maybe I won't. But I'll shoot for it. Just talking it out will make me feel better—always does.

It really isn't the job. It's me, and people and remembering that I have to always keep working on my addictions. Maybe that's what coping is all about—people making it, and me making it with me.

Now let's see. Where did I put that hammer?

II. AN ESSENTIAL PRINCIPLE FOR TRUE INTIMACY:

People need agreement. They are in such fear of not getting it that they are afraid to step forward and say what is going on inside, what is true for them. Unless they can come from truth, intimacy is impossible.

A Typical Problem in Life which Frustrates Us:

You just saw a movie. The reviews were great. Everybody has been raving about the movie. But your reaction to it was that it was a monumental bore, a total waste of time. While you're sitting in a group, the movie is brought up.

The Unintimate Reaction:
Others: We saw that movie, yesterday.
You: Oh, I saw that movie too.
Others: What did you think of it?
You: Oh...er...it was great!
Others: The special effects, the color, they were fantastic. That movie has to win an Oscar.
You: (*Warming up to the subject*) Yeah. Fantastic special effects. Did you see the way they had that rocket ship take off and the picture of the earth disappearing into the background? Really great!

Others: (*A long pause*) The story was a little confusing...it seemed to drag at times.
You: Yeah. What was the point of the movie, anyway?

The Intimate Person:
Others: We saw that movie, yesterday.
You: Oh, I saw that movie too.
Others: What did you think of it?
You: It was terrible. I found it so boring I fell asleep. What a bomb!
Others: Gee, I'm glad you said that. Everyone is raving about it. I was afraid I'd seem a little—er—out of it if I said it was lousy. Now that you said it, I have to ask: how could the critics have given it the reviews they did?
You: (*Laughing*) I don't know.
Others: Funny thing is that nobody ever said they hated it. But look at us now. Seems nobody in this room liked it. Isn't it great to be able to be honest with each other?
You: Yep. We're all afraid to be wrong.
Others: How come you admitted you didn't like it? It didn't seem to bother you at *all* that we might not agree.
You: I like to say what's so for me. To just come from truth. I have found

	that if I don't do that, if I worry about being wrong, I have a tight stomach or a headache or something.
Others:	I always worry that I'll look like a smart ass.
You:	I used to worry about that too. But I find that if you don't make the others wrong, just acknowledge their point of view, they'll be ready to listen to your opinion.
Others:	Just imagine how many groups, even mobs, have people in it who are afraid to be wrong and just follow the crowd? It's amazing. Well, I'll say what's so for me right now. I'm hungry. I'm also tired of this conversation. Let's go eat.
You:	That's cool. Let's go.

They leave. The unintimate one, the one who provided the unintimate reaction is upset. He thinks to himself:

I really hated that movie. Why couldn't I say it? I'm always afraid to say what I really feel. Funny, I feel so tight right now that my stomach is hurting. I even have a slight headache. Oh hell. Why does everyone make me so uptight?

Wish I could be like John (*or Mary*). He (*she*) seems to get away with things like that, saying what they really feel, and people don't jump on them. He says lots of things I wish I could say. People seem to like it when he steps forward. I hate to admit it, but I like when he does it too. I'll bet he doesn't get a headache, tight stomach or dry mouth as often as I do.

III. AN ESSENTIAL PRINCIPLE FOR TRUE INTIMACY

Staying in the reality of the here and now. Remembering that since you can only steer your own ship when you are at choice, you want to pick preferences to get out of the addicted level. And then move towards those preferences knowing that you win some and you lose some. But at the preference level it's acceptable. At the addicted level it is intolerable.

A Typical Problem in Life which Frustrates Us:

You are attending an important function. You have laid out your best clothes. It's late but there is just enough time to make it. As you begin to get dressed you discover that the zipper in your trousers or dress is broken.

The Unintimate Reaction:

*!#%!!! Every time I need something I find nothing but incompetence all around me. That Goddamned (*store, tailor, wife, husband, dressmaker, WORLD*) should have

seen this zipper was broken. I'm so mad now I'd like to rip this thing into shreds. What am I going to do? What can I wear? I was really looking forward to wearing this. And it cost a fortune.

Why does this always happen to me? I'm going to tell that——off. Kicking that chair felt good. Oh, God, the leg just broke and it cracked the glass on the antique display case. What else can happen to me? I'd like to put my fist through the wall. (*He/she screams loudly for whoever is there—wife, husband, whoever—to get his/her ass in that room, pronto, and give him/her a hand.*)

The Intimate Reaction:

*!#%!!! Well, this is a hell of a situation. I feel like ripping this thing to shreds. Look at me—I'm so angry I'm shaking. Easy now—look at this emotional thing you're going through. I think I hear the Brat, the Collector and the Manipulator all laughing hysterically. Well, it sure isn't what I wanted. What's the reality? The zipper broke. I guess that's what's so. What's the best way to handle *this* in the here and now?

Well, it happened. What's my preference? I can't fix it, that's for sure. No time. I could call the whole thing off, but I really want to go. Guess I'll have to wear something else. Who is to blame for this? What's the difference? It happened, that's all.

(*He/she calls out for whoever is there—parent, lover, friend, wife, husband—whoever.*)

Guess what? I pulled a beauty here. Maybe I yanked too hard on it. I don't know. But I got this zipper stuck. I really felt my buttons being pressed for a while there—got myself into a beauty of an addiction. But that won't get me to that function. I might as well change. What do you think I ought to wear?

IV. AN ESSENTIAL PRINCIPLE FOR TRUE INTIMACY

Acknowledging the other person's point of view. Remembering there is no chance for intimacy if you make the other person wrong. Taking responsibility for whatever happens.

A Typical Problem in Life which Frustrates Us:

You are trying to make an important call, and keep getting a busy signal. Or nobody answers at all.

The Unintimate Reaction:

Dammit! Where the hell is he/she? I've been trying this phone all day and all I get is busy signals or no answer. What's going on? They knew I was going to call! I can't stand so many inconsiderate people in this world. Why didn't she keep the line open?

People just don't seem to give a damn. What do they think—that I have nothing better to do all day but sit on this phone?

(*Tries the call again. Busy. Bangs phone down in its cradle, and calls the operator.*)

Person: Hello, operator?
Operator: Yes?
Person: I've been calling this number all day. What the hell is wrong with these phones?
Operator: (*slight edge to her voice*) Sometimes the circuits are busy, sir, and...
Person: All day? Come on!
Operator: I'm sorry you're having so much trouble sir. If you want I...
Person: Why don't you check it out? This is an important call.
Operator: What's the number, sir? (*Pause*) I'm sorry, it's busy.
Person: Well, this is important. Just cut in.
Operator: I'm sorry, we can't do that.
Person: You mean you *won't*. I don't think you people know what you're doing. If they had competent people handling these jobs we wouldn't have all these problems. I think you people..hello, hello, HELLO. I don't believe it. That bitch hung up!

The Intimate Reaction:
Person: Dammit! The phone is still busy. I'd better check with the operator.
Operator: Yes?
Person: I have a real problem here, operator.
Operator: Yes?
Person: Operator, I've been trying this number all day, and it's always busy. I have a really important call to make, here, and I'm really upset.
Operator: (*Understandingly*) I understand. How long have you been trying it?
Person: A long time, operator.
Operator: What is the number? (*Pause*) It's busy, sir.
Person: I don't know what to do. You must run into this thing all the time and I'm sure you know the best thing to do. What do you suggest?
Operator: Let's check the verifying operator.
(*Verifying operator, after checking it, reports that they are speaking on the phone*)
Person: I hate to be a pest, but...
Operator: Did you say it was an emergency?

Person: Welll...no, not that kind of emergency.
Operator: Because in emergency situations we can cut in.
Person: (*Eagerly*) Oh? Would you do that?
Operator: It's irregular, but I guess we can do that. (*Pause*) You can call now. The phone is clear.
Person: Oh, wonderful. How can I thank you?
Operator: No problem at all. Wish more people were as understanding as you, and that people wouldn't blame the operators and the phone company all the time. I just hung up on someone who was really nasty!

V. AN ESSENTIAL PRINCIPLE FOR TRUE INTIMACY

Reality is agreement. We create our own reality. When we do that we can get the cheese.

A Typical Problem in Life which Frustrates Us:

He wants to make love and the girl says no. She wants to make love and the fellow is too tired or just indifferent.

The Most Unintimate Reaction:

He: Wanna fuck?
She: No. Not when you approach me like that.
He: Dammit. Fuck you.

The Typical Unintimate Reaction:
He/She: You and your headaches! You're always tired. I'm going to trade you in for a new model. If you gave a damn about me and didn't always just think of yourself you'd do something about it. You're a selfish bastard/bitch. It'll be a long time before I turn to you again.

The Intimate Reaction:
He: Honey?
She: Yes?
He: I feel sexy.
She: Gosh. I don't feel too well/am tired/have a headache, etc.
He: I want to share with you what happens inside of me at times like this. I mean it really presses my buttons.
She: I'm sorry, dear.
He: Well, I guess I don't feel like it at times either.
She: Could we let it go tonight?
He: Sure, honey. I'll survive. (*laughs*)

She: (*After a pause.*) You're wonderful. You never make me feel like a louse when I'm just not into sex. Thanks for being so understanding.
He: Why should you feel like a louse? After all, honey, like they say, when you're hot you're hot and when you're not you're not.
She: You know, with more men like you men and women would get along so much better.
He: Oh, come on. Anybody can understand that there are times...
She: But honey...
He: Yes?
She: How do you figure it?
He: Figure what?
She: Now I feel in the mood too. Isn't that something?
He: (*Holding her close.*) Mmmmm. I guess it proves one thing.
She: What's that?
He: Don't make the other person wrong, don't invade their body-bubble, and then good things can happen.
She: (*Purring*) Yes, dear. One good thing is about to happen right now.
He: What's that?
She: It's going to be okay to invade my body-bubble right now.

VI. AN ESSENTIAL PRINCIPLE FOR TRUE INTIMACY

Knowing that you have done what others have done. That's compassion.

*A Typical Problem in Life
which Frustrates Us:*

You are on the highway. Suddenly someone cuts into your lane, unexpectedly, and you have to brake sharply to avoid hitting him.

The Unintimate Reaction:

That son of a bitch! What kind of driving is that? (*He steps on the gas, pulls alongside the other car, lowers his window and screams at the driver*)

"What the hell do you think you're doing? Do you know you almost ripped my fender off?" (*The rest of the screaming the reader can easily fill in, for we have all had our buttons pressed, moved into our addictions, and run our act through as robots. How will it end? At the least with ugly looks. At the worst, they may both pull over to the shoulder and you may read about it in the newspaper the next day.*)

The Intimate Reaction:

Wow! He nearly tore my fender off. I can feel my buttons being pressed because my first urge is to catch up to him and really tell him off. What am I feeling now? It's a beauty of an addiction. Is my head throbbing and is my heart pounding!

I hear you, Manipulator. Those tapes are really bringing back other times when I felt pushed around and impotent. If I listen to you I'd catch up to the other guy and give him hell.

Let's take that pause for a second. Right now I think I'm above the addiction. You know, *I've* done the same thing plenty of times. But I always forgave myself when *I* did it.

What's my preference? Well, I would have preferred that it didn't happen because he really shook me up. The reality of the here and now? It happened. I'll shoot for my preference which is to share with him how it felt when he did it. (*He pulls up to the other car, which has stopped for a light, and lowers his window. Putting both hands up, palms upward, he says with a smile:*)

He: What happened back there? That was pretty close.
Other: I'm sorry. I'm rushing to the hospital. (*Or, I didn't realize we were so close. Or, sorry, I was daydreaming. Or, whatever.*)
He: Okay. Be careful. It's not worth killing yourself. Or someone else.
Other: I guess so. Thanks for being so understanding. So long.

VII. AN ESSENTIAL PRINCIPLE FOR TRUE INTIMACY

Knowing that being right, being reasonable, even being righteous is just following the old tapes and going through your act.

*A Typical Problem in Life
which Frustrates Us:*

You are in a restaurant. The waitress appears to have ignored you. You are hungry. It seems that people who have come in after you have already been served.

The Unintimate Reaction:

Damn it! What kind of service is this? I'm starving, and the goddamned waitress seems to be in a fog. I've had enough of this—I'm going to talk to the manager.

He: Look, we've been waiting for a long time for service. The waitress just ignores us.

Manager: Who is your waitress, sir?

He: That one, the redhead.

Manager: Mary, this gentleman has been waiting for service for a long time.

Waitress: I'm sorry, sir, but we've been terribly busy. We're just short handed.

Manager: Sir, two waitresses called in sick.

He: Well, you should tell the cus-

	tomers they will have to wait for a long time. We're leaving.
Manager:	I'm sorry, sir.
He:	(*Leaving*) And don't expect us back here again!

The Intimate Reaction:

Damn it! What kind of service is this? I really feel ignored. What am I feeling besides that? I hear the voice of the Brat telling me I'm hungry and the voice of the Manipulator telling me not to let them get away with it.

What's the reality of the here and now? They seem terribly busy. Seems like they are short of help or something. Which is our waitress? Oh, there she is. The fat redhead. Funny how fat redhaired women affect me. Wonder what that's all about? I seem to go into my Manipulated Act around redhaired women. Especially when they ignore me. Oh, well.

I had thought of leaving. Talking to the manager. But I'm better off talking to myself and going towards preferences has gotten me out of my addiction. What's my preference? That that nice blonde kid wait on us. She seems friendly and seems to be a better waitress. I lost that preference all right. I guess I'm stuck. (*He looks around, studies the decor of the restaurant, notices the different people, and involves himself in*

113

conversation with the other people at his table. Eventually he gets the waitress' attention and she comes over.)

Waitress: I'm sorry, sir. We've been short handed. Two girls called in sick.

He: Yes. I guess that happens. I'm sure it's not your fault. But we're really starving. Could you serve us as soon as possible?

Waitress: (*Taking the order*) Of course, sir. I wish others were as understanding. It's not an easy job—and everybody blames the waitress. You know what? One man just walked out angry as the devil.
What can I bring you?

He: The cheese. (*laughs*) No. That's just a little joke. Has to do with getting the rewards in life. Now let's see. I think I'd like some...

VIII. AN ESSENTIAL PRINCIPLE FOR TRUE INTIMACY

Don't judge behavior. Just react to it with your honest feelings about what's so for you when such behavior occurs.

Two Typical Problems in Life which Frustrate Us:

Problem 1: You have had an appointment. The other person shows up 35 minutes late.

Problem 2: You have caught your child in a blatant lie.

The Unintimate Reaction—Problem 1:
"Do you know how long I've been waiting? You're 35 minutes late!"
"I'm sorry, but I just couldn't get away. And then the traffic was horrendous. I just misjudged how long it would take."
"You know how it feels to just sit/stand and wait? Dammit, I always keep my appointments. I'm always on time."
(*Sarcastically*) "Well, I guess you're just a better person than I am."

The Intimate Reaction—Problem 1:
"What happened?"
"I'm sorry, but I just couldn't get away. And then the traffic was horrendous. I just misjudged how long it would take."
"I know. I've had that happen to me too. I was worried about you. I'm glad that you're okay and nothing happened."
"Thanks for being understanding. I felt lousy because I know how it is to just sit/stand and wait."
"Well, guess we better get going. Know what happened at the office today? Well, this fellow Marty..."

The Unintimate Reaction—Problem 2:
"You know that's not true! That's a lie! Why don't you be a man and admit it?"

"It's true!"

"You're nothing but a lousy liar! You make me sick."

The Intimate Reaction—Problem 2:
"You know that's not true!"

"It's true!"

"You know how I feel when I know you are lying? I feel sad, and I take responsibility for it. I just wish you didn't have to be so afraid that you couldn't trust me with the truth."

"Gee, I'm sorry you feel that way..."

"Well, I have to share with you how disappointed I am at these times."

(*Pause*) "Well, what really happened was..."

Once the threat of being wrong, of being judged, and then having to defend against the onslaught of righteousness which others heap on at those moments—once that is past, the other person can now deal with your problem.

The real problem? So many of us suffer from a terminal case of hardening of the attitudes.

IX. AN ESSENTIAL PRINCIPLE FOR TRUE INTIMACY:

Don't pigeonhole others. Don't keep them stuck in the same old position. Allow for change, don't get fixed in the old sameness in your point of view about others. You can actually be grateful when others can give you a chance to work on your addictions. No other person can give you a pain in the neck. Only *you* can do that to yourself.

*A Typical Problem in Life
which Frustrates Us:*

You are planning to go to a party. You discover that someone you have never liked is going to be there.

The Unintimate Reaction:

Forget it! I'm not going! Never could stand him/her. I couldn't have a good time with him/her there. John/Mary knows I can't stand him/her. Why the hell would they do such a stupid thing as inviting him/her when they know I'm coming to the party? I feel like calling them up and telling them off for inviting that creep to the party when they knew I was coming.

The Intimate Reaction:

He/she has been invited to the party. There was a time, before I understood my addictions, that I would never go to that party. I used to hear the Brat telling me that my evening would be ruined, the Collector telling me that I never felt secure around him/her, and the Manipulator telling me that he/she is much too forceful and makes me feel pressured in his/her company.

I remember when I would say he/she gave me a pain in the neck. Now I know I gave myself a pain in the neck when I was with him/her. I have to take responsibility for that.

Well, I'll have a real opportunity to work on my addictions, and not pigeonhole him/her into the same old slots, playing out the same old roles from my tapes. I'm going to look at this get-together as a chance to work on my addictions. I'm not going to run from this situation. My preference used to be that such people wouldn't be there. But I guess I lose this one. I prefer to go to the party and I'll move towards that one. I'd like to think I've reached the point where I'm grateful for him/her for the opportunity he/she gives me to work on my addictions.

X. AN ESSENTIAL PRINCIPLE FOR TRUE INTIMACY

Taking the significance out of "what's out there."

A Typical Problem in Life
which Frustrates Us:

I'm in a rush, and find that I'm caught in a terrible traffic jam.

The Unintimate Reaction:

If they had built these roads like they should have this wouldn't happen. Why the hell is that guy in front of me creeping like that? Yes, you! Yeah! I'm honking my horn at you! Wake up, you jerk. Move it!

I feel like exploding. I had these plans for today, and I have this tight schedule and I'm stuck in this crazy traffic jam. It's important stuff. The majority of these people are just loafing around, probably just joyriding or going shopping. Dammit, move it, buddy! I haven't got all day!

The Intimate Reaction:

Will you just look at this traffic jam! This is the kind of frustrating situation which used to bring out all my addictions. I remember how I used to scream at the drivers to move it, and I would keep honking my horn. The Manipulator and the Brat would be buzzing in my head, taunting me. The Collector was the worst. I equated getting there on time with my whole security bit.

I made the whole thing significant at those times. I see that now. The big deals, the schedules, the appointments. The only significance they had was what I gave them. I really created that reality when I defended my notions to the death.

Oh, well. I guess I won't get my preferences in *this* here and now. I sure won't get there at nine as I had hoped. May as well enjoy what I can. Interesting billboard that. Never saw the sun as orange as that.

Where are we now? Oh, at the Main Street intersection. I've never been stuck here before. Oh, that poor guy in the next car. Look at him honking his horn! He's really addicted. Yes, he's really running his act through, and is *he* ever a robot right now! If he's the way I used to be, I'll bet he thinks what he has to do today is *very* significant, that he's into very important stuff and that we're all just loafing around, joyriding or shopping. I know that feeling. Had it all the time.

Why am I caught in this traffic jam? Not for any reasons the Manipulator and the Brat and the Collector would like to have me think. This really has nothing to do with my tapes, unless I really start to go along with all the old beliefs. I know better today. I know why I'm caught in this traffic jam. Because I *am* caught in this traffic jam. Period.

XI. AN ESSENTIAL PRINCIPLE FOR TRU TRUE INTIMACY:

What you experience is the truth. What you believe is a lie.

A Typical Problem in Life which Frustrates Us

Sitting with people who don't believe that what you experience is the truth, and what you believe is a lie. And watching them go through their act.

The Unintimate Reaction:

What do I feel? What a lot of shit. I feel with my fingers. How's that for an answer?

You keep asking what I'm experiencing. About what? Why don't you come off it with this "here and now" stuff? When I feel something, believe me people know. If I get mad enough I tell people off and sometimes I punch people in the nose. How's that for feelings? (*laughs*)

What? You say experience is the only truth, and that all my beliefs are lies? What the hell is *that* supposed to mean? Right now I'll tell you what I believe. I believe you're putting me on. Keep pushing me and you'll have a real experience. Watching me explode.

The Intimate Reaction:

(now that you have read this far, isn't this *your* reaction?)

What do I feel? I feel uptight.

Yes, I know you feel uptight at times, too. We all do. And angry. Didn't my questions get you angry? They did? You were getting a headache? Why didn't you say *that*?

There was no point to it? Sure there was.

It didn't need a reason. It didn't need understanding. It just was. You felt it and that made it so. That's what was true for you—that headache.

You see, the minute, the split-second it happens, that's what your experience is. All the rest are the beliefs you had about that experience. They're lies, those beliefs. The only thing that was true was that split second you experienced yourself.

Look at it like this. If all your beliefs, everything on your tapes since you were born were beads, strung out on an endless string, the first bead on that string would be each new experience. The rest of the beads after that first one are just your beliefs about that experience.

Now if you took a scissors, kept only that first bead on the string, the actual experience itself, and cut the rest of the beads off—all those beliefs about that experience, what would you have?

That's right. You'd have just the one bead, the split-second experience itself. Letting go of the other beads is what it's all about. If you let them go, all of them, you'd be left with your Self. Just you.

I see you are smiling. It is a nice thought, isn't it. Just you, just your Self. Without all that crap we call our beliefs which we carry around with us all day. Without all those beliefs we are just like we came into this world—pretty perfect.

Easy? Who ever said it was easy? It's damned tough. How do you get in touch with your insides? Just listen to what is going on inside you. Feel it the instant it happens. Separate that experience from the beliefs which will flash at you almost as instantaneously as the beliefs.

I did it again? I used that word experience again? Yep. I know. By the way. What did you experience when I used that word *experience* again?

Chapter 4

Sexual Intimacy—The Sexual Athlete

Now that we have explored what intimacy and non-intimacy consist of; now that we have some understanding of the steps that have to be taken to become an intimate person, we are ready to look at *another* kind of intimacy: sexual intimacy.

Sexual intimacy stands apart from ordinary people intimacy. It's terribly important to be able to talk to that telephone operator and to get along with that person you couldn't tolerate in the past. But you don't expect to have sexual intimacy with the gas station attendant or the butcher or your co-worker or the fellow in the next car in that ubiquitous traffic jam.

Sexual intimacy calls for a prerequisite—*people intimacy*. There is little doubt about that. Until we can follow the steps outlined in part one, there can't be *any* intimacy. But it is very possible to be an intimate person with the grocer or the waitress and still not be a sexually intimate person. For that, the extra steps which have to be taken call for being naked-naked. It means taking chances and facing the danger of stripping away the armor, getting rid of the barriers and crossing some *extra* bridges.

The man who represents the greatest barrier to true male-female sexual intimacy is the one who has come to be known as the Jock—the Sexual Athlete.

The Sexual Athlete

Look how big I am.
Where?
Where? Where do you think.
Oh, there.

Look at the muscles.
The hair on my chest.
The back muscles.

Where?

Where? Where do you think.
All over is muscle.
Oh, there.

You're not looking!
What's the matter with you?
Why aren't you looking?
Doesn't that magnificent tool
Make you feel fantastic?

Fantastic.

You're still not looking.
What stops you from sharing all this?
With me.

My loneliness.

We appear to be enjoying a huge amount of sexual freedom today. It wasn't always so. It was Kinsey who rocked the sexual complacency of our culture over a quarter century ago. Even *he* was stunned by the furor his findings created.

Kinsey, after all, had written a tome—a classical sociological study of the sexual behavior of the human male. Subsequently, he followed up his original study with an in-depth exploration of the sexual habits of the female. He put a spotlight on sensitive areas of sexuality which had, up to that time, been associated with shame, guilt and secrecy. As a scientist, he simply reported his findings which covered a wide range of sexual human behavior including marital and pre-marital sex, petting to achieve orgasm, and frequency of orgasm. The startling nature of the research—which showed that men and women enjoyed sexual activities of a far wider range than had been recognized—galvanized the American public into a new excitement and curiosity concerning sex and the human animal.

Social scientists and other professionals began to interpret and make judgments about Kinsey's straightforward and clinical studies. A huge volume of literature was published in response to the phenomenal public interest in the new sexology. We experienced the greatest sexual revolution the average man in the street could recall. It was anarchy, and by far the finest example of sexual heresy since Freud's theories in the early 1920's.

The American woman was shocked by the knowledge that it was now desired—indeed, expected—that she enjoy a level of sexual gratification unknown to the average woman before that time. She was totally inundated by all forms of media which lost no opportunity to remind her that frequent and satisfying orgasms and a passionate sexual response were her inalienable rights, and her husband's most sacred duties. In the years immediately following the Kinsey research, she was asked to put aside the cultural and sexual heritage which had been carefully nurtured for centuries, and feel free in expecting—even demanding—equal and mutual sexual satisfaction. The implications of this were enormous. After all, hadn't sexual gratification been essentially reserved for the Male? Wasn't it the female role to supply sexual pleasure with little concern for her own enjoyment? Wasn't the aggressive and passionate female usually looked upon with suspicion and even scorn? Wouldn't sexual experimentation on her part make her seem promiscuous or even perverted? Now, she was being told to set aside these very serious issues which women had always faced in preceding generations, and adopt a free and aggressive sexual role which stressed that orgasms were required for her to consider herself a complete woman.

Intellectually she was happy to take on the role of the sexually responsive woman; culturally and traditionally she was quite unprepared for it. She was caught in a deadly crossfire: keeping up with the current cultural demands which would give her pleasure at the expense of her religious and early childhood training.

The man, of course, was not aware of what was happening. He was pleased to think of his sexual partner as a sexually stimulating—and stimulated—woman. It fit not only his fantasies of the Sensual

Woman, it made his dream of a passionate and active partner appear near fruition. Valiantly he entered into the spirit of The Game. It was not long before he was caught in the same deadly cultural-masculine-heritage kind of crossfire.

It soon became apparent that this new role as Lover was going to be a difficult one. Questions now arose to plague him. What if he couldn't perform as well as might be expected? Hadn't he always enjoyed sex when and as the mood struck him without too much concern for the girl's ability to climax? What if she *couldn't* climax? Wasn't the ideal partner one who put her sexual pleasures aside and considered man's pleasures as fundamental to her?

The new demands on him soon found him tense and anxious under the pressures to perform and satisfy. An orgasm-focused cult rapidly developed. Concern about determining better ways of satisfying the female became a paramount issue for the male. At that point man and woman were faced with a conflict they had never really been confronted with before.

Dr. Kinsey's remarkable study had opened up a new world in the area of sex. It was suddenly a time when people could talk openly and freely about previously forbidden areas of sexuality. It became passé to consider anything perverted between two consenting adults engaging in a mutually satisfying sexual act. New possibilities for sophisticated humor revolving around sexual themes were seen. What had but a short time before been considered "dirty" and "shameful" and "immoral" was now being discussed openly in forums, on University campuses, and women's clubs across the nation. Guests on radio programs and television panel shows were now informing us all that we had had our heads buried for far too long. The pulpit became a sounding board for urging frankness and honesty in sexual discussions.

What a marvelous opportunity in man's rather sordid sexual history to develop a better understanding of the respective feelings and sexual attitudes of both men and women!

For the first time in many years we were laughing openly about what had previously been sacred in sex. A real chance to achieve closeness based on tolerance of sexuality emerged. Our humor in the early 1950's reflects this:

Lord Chesterfield, who lived in the 18th century, was being widely quoted and paraphrased at this time. One example was a letter to his son:

Son, here is the money you asked for since you left for London. Spend

> *it wisely. One thing I would tell you about sex: it is time consuming, dangerous to your health, and, above all, the positions are ridiculous.*

America listened to such sacrilege. And America laughed.

Dorothy Parker's poetry of the 1920's was suddenly popular again for it reflected the new acceptance about attitudes the sexes have always had towards each other:

> By the time you swear you're his
> Shivering and sighing,
> And he vows his passion is
> Infinite, undying,
> One of you is lying.

America continued to chuckle. Even the derivation of the word "fuck" was now talked about in a new social context:

F   U   C   K

For Unlawful Carnal Knowledge

Is that what the derivation was? For Unlawful Carnal Knowledge? That dreaded word which made men explode and women grow faint? We smiled, and relaxed a bit more.

Yes, we had our bid for closeness and with such openness and laughter the possibilities for a true sexual intimacy existed as never before. We had a chance for the Blue Bird, the Rainbow, the Golden Opportunity.

We could have seen the sexes reunited as in that myth by Plato, powerful in our wholeness and oneness once again. From such union would have emerged a man who could be tender, aware of the female which resides within him and unthreatened by it. Hadn't Plato pointed out that when man was aware of both the male and female within himself he was strong and powerful? Instead, man turned away from the enormous implications of such a man-woman union and spawned a totally different type of symbol which didn't stress closeness, but emphasized performance, competition, keeping score cards and practicing.

The professional literature which interpreted Kinsey, and later the media—movies, television, magazines, books and newspapers—had taken the research findings, extrapolated the more dramatic and sensational aspects of his erudite study, dressed it for mass consumption and reinterpreted it to make it eminently readable. Being culture-bound, they had taken from the study what had impressed them most: that women needed to be sexually satisfied to a greater degree than ever before. They simply didn't see the possibilities for true intimacy in these new dimensions of female sexuality.

The media had completely missed the point when they placed emphasis on orgiastic release and frenetic foreplay. What happened was that the man in the street bought the whole package: not an appeal for intimacy but a cleverly packaged and dressed up series of "how to" sex manuals.

Van de Velde had taught generations of newlyweds about foreplay and orgasms for decades. There was nothing new in that. What was *not* needed was more rationalization for a new and increased form of sex play. A relationship focused on sexual performance shut the door to any possibilities of bringing the sexes closer.

With that door to frank self-introspection closed, competitiveness to catch up with our neighbors began in earnest. A new *nonintimacy age* began. The rest is history. If humor is ultimately pathos, it took on a Keystone Kops frenzy. America stopped laughing. We stopped chuckling goodnaturedly, and our smiles became forced. What had initially been a jovial sprint became a deadly serious "let's catch up" race.

We never really understood or interpreted correctly the basic research. If we had, we would have seen that women don't just want release: they want closeness. Orgasm without tender and gentle touch would have been seen as empty and hollow. The man didn't understand this; the woman herself didn't realize it at that point. Swept up in the fervor of the New Sexology, we spawned an emotionless sexual competitor who earned laurels and racked up points which could be measured by sighs, groans and orgasms. Our dilemma: we were caught between the terror of intimacy and the horror of loneliness.

We emphasized a part of the male—concern for performance and prowess and muscles. What emerged from the research ruins was not a return to the Platonic wholeness theme which made men and women so strong in their unity, or the drollness of Chesterfieldian humor which made us laugh at ourselves, but an anomaly, a machine-like performer known as *the sexual athlete*.

Who is this man we are calling the Sexual Athlete? The sex jock? Clearly he is not one man, for he is a composite of qualities which reside in all men when they equate manhood with virility and strength. He is the arch-enemy of true intimacy, for in his equating performance with manhood he can never experience closeness. Men who use him as a symbol—the one to emulate—are following a non-intimate idol. The degree to which he is seen as the Real Man, will determine his disciples' emotional isolation, be he a Caspar Milquetoast or a Don Juan.

The Sexual Athlete is very serious about the role of sex in his life. He studies it. He plans it. He constantly rehearses to reach a more perfect level of competence. This unique athlete has to prove his prowess in bed no less than other athletes have to master the track or the gridiron or the tennis court. Where others do push-ups he masters the pelvic thrust; to him deep breathing exercises relate to sexual intercourse. He is always in training. New postures and positions and sexual experiences are a challenge to his ingenuity. Once mastered they are seen as notches carved in his pistol.

He doesn't think of love, but of being *a Lover*. His goal is to produce orgasms and to involve the woman as much as possible in the sex act while holding back his total involvement as much as possible. He measures closeness and intimacy with a woman in terms of the bodies touching rather than the spirits, and he checks his timing and endurance as diligently as any trainer with a stop-watch clocking a yearling. Because he is oriented to giving pleasure, and because he feels he exhibits great concern for the female during the sex act, he deceives himself into thinking he has a highly intimate relationship with women, when in reality he is only erotically acquainted. Other men who are equally performance-oriented see him as the Standard Bearer of Masculinity. The degree to which a man is not in touch with the Self, the greater the emphasis on scorekeeping, the greater the tendency to emulate and deify rather than defy the sexual jock.

Since the Sexual Athlete is essentially a performer he has a sense of the dramatic, a flair for the spotlight equal to that of any actor. He places great emphasis on strength, on "keeping in shape" and on keeping himself sexually attractive.

He develops a jargon and sets up a highly personalized lexicon. He refers to his sex life in terms of his ability to "perform" well. In a more solemn mood he may speak of it as the "sex act." How interesting that he sees it as "performing" and "acting"! Rarely does he speak of "loving." Intercourse is spoken of as "balling." When a woman yields to him—even his wife—he counts points and speaks of her acquiescence in terms of his "scoring."

Scoring clearly spells out the name of the game, and his concentration on points. Like Willie Mays he says, "If you don't care about winning why keep score?" He cares. He watches. He keeps score. And he ultimately becomes a spectator-player. (The sports athlete—baseball player, boxer, etc.—says it's the legs which give out first. To the sex athlete what gives out first is of grave concern too.)

To him, women are "birds," "chicks," or a "piece." He sees himself as the Guardian of the Piece, for he truly believes that he can bring ultimate ecstacy to any female. He is a master at the game of foreplay. (Interestingly enough, the word "foreplay," which contains the word "play" within it, is a singularly unilateral word, for it is the only one in the English language all of us use when referring to preliminaries to sexual intercourse. In some ways, then, we are all playing the game.)

The Sexual Athlete refers to his penis as "Charlie," or "The Peter." In a more flamboyant mood, he may speak of it as "the magnificent tool." He is convinced that Peter needs constant workouts to keep its strength and durability.

Schopenhauer referred to such people as analogous to the porcupines who huddle together for warmth. As they press together, their quills stick each other, and they are forced to pull apart. Once apart they begin to freeze again. Again and again they will try to press against each other for warmth, only to feel the quills and part again. In the fable, this went on all night, and the two of them were found in the morning, frozen to death.

Intimacy was impossible for the porcupines because of the painful stabbing of the quills. The Sexual Athlete has his own set of quills for protection. But he has gone one step beyond the porcupine: his quills are invisible and don't show how they are stabbing the partner. They just hold her off, never allowing true emotional closeness. That is integral to his relationship.

A society such as ours is grist for the Sexual Athlete's mill. It is built upon competitive values and supported by an affluent economic structure. From the original Horatio Alger fable we have progressed—or regressed, depending upon the point of view—to a phenomenon called "testing the limits" by psychoanalysts, "upmanship" by social scientists, and "how far can we go" by the man in the street. Such a culture makes one man's sexual freedom another man's indecency, and still another man's fast buck. The Sexual Athlete's survival is insured when performance is implanted in us almost from birth. That is why, at the Kinsey Crossroads, it was so easy for us to follow the Performance Parade instead of the road which was an Invitation to Intimacy.

The American Performer gets his start very early in life. For his wide-eyed-wonder-at-the-world look, the baby receives rewards which fall into the "I-think-we-have-a-genius-here" classification. Later he will be asked to sing that cute song or recite that little poem for Aunt Clara. In kindergarten we find a mad scramble takes place to produce "reading readiness," and superior scholastic performance becomes a sine qua non for pleasing parents and teachers. The expected quid pro quo: smiles of recognition, acceptance, and regard for the performance. Little boys join Little League and forever after will make the one who excells in sports the Popular One. Their fathers will throw footballs and baseballs at them for hours on end. Later, throughout high school and college, a young man with a strong throwing arm or the ability to put a ball through a hoop can still find he is the Big Man on Campus. His apprenticeship for the Corporate Structure allows him to keep putting sales and profits through hoops to remain the BMOC with the President of the Company.

Whether the child wants all this from the very outset appears merely incidental. He is dictated to from the beginning, and he spends his whole life performing stunts for his masters: mom and pop, teachers—indeed, anyone who can tap his fears of failure or reach in and touch his innermost needs for success. In time the child learns what not to hear, what not to see, what not to touch, and even which feelings to have. These teachings are programmed into his brain like punch cards into a computer. As adults we can learn how to pull out of the Performance Parade. As parents we can finally realize that it is up to us to make sure our child doesn't line up for the parade. One thing is certain: we don't *have to* keep using the same old punch cards with the same old punch holes which were put there at the beginning! We *know* how those tapes perpetrate non-intimacy.

We are the co-authors of our life style. We collaborated with so many people along the way who contributed, but it is our autobiography and we must do the final editing. One day—sooner or later—a man reaches a crossroads and has a major decision to make. In terms of happy and fulfilling interpersonal relationships it is probably the most important decision he will ever make. The choices are clear enough. He can follow the Pied Piper of Performance if he fears that to do otherwise will result in having his medals discarded, his buttons ripped off, his epaulets torn away and his Sword of Masculinity broken or perhaps just bent. In that case, to the slow beat of the drums he will find himself non-intimate and eventually banished to the Siberia of Emotional Isolation.

The intimate man, however, can realize that he is a man and not a robot, that the punch cards were put there, but that he keeps computerizing and reprogramming himself. In that case he can avoid the quills of Schopenhauer's porcupines, find strength through the unity of the sexes which Plato spoke of and finally know what Buddha meant when he said that he was awake. He can then step out behind the shower door which in its opaqueness only lets us know that someone is there but that we really mustn't see him naked.

He can choose the road to follow. It can be the Invitation to Intimacy or the road to Non-Intimate Isolation. Should he choose non-intimacy, his lovemaking will remain a mindless venture into seeing which anatomical buttons he can press to produce the greatest ecstacies and—still striving for pinnacles—hope to continue rewards for his success. Perplexed, he will wonder why the increases in sexual ingenuity don't bring man closer to woman. Instead, intimacy will get lost along the way and he will find himself a beggar at the feast.

Here are some of the typical anti-intimate types of personality profiles which the sexual athlete develops. I present five sketches just to illustrate them—although ten times as many could be described. The formula is simple in all of them: the focus on competition and performance will increase the orgasms but decrease any chances for true intimacy between a man and a woman.

Case 1: The Show Off

Harry has an attractive wife. He is very proud of her, and makes it apparent that he feels she is beautiful. What *she* feels is that she is a showcase, a label, a beautiful possession to be displayed. She tries to look beautiful at all times, for she knows how it affects him mentally and physically. When she looks particularly well he beams. At night, when she gets ready for bed, she puts on a seductive negligee and parades in front of him. He leans back on the bed and becomes aroused as he watches her and reflects on how his friends must envy him. They then have what Harry calls "fantastic sex." A few times when she wasn't feeling well, or when she didn't look stunning, Harry acted disappointed, sulked, and ultimately appeared depressed. Those nights there was a strain between them. There was no fantastic sex. There was no sex at all.

Harry must win in the Spouse Sweepstakes. Competition with other men is the stimulus for his sexual arousal. He used to show off his marble collection, his bicycle, his new car. He has never stopped competing. Unfortunately, his wife knows that she will have to stay in the Gorgeous Game for as long as she can.

Her secret fear: Harry will divorce her when she gets old and find a young, attractive wife.

Case 2: The Financial Fornicator

Tom is a salesman. When he makes a sale, or receives a big bonus, it is matched by erections. There is a direct one-to-one relationship between orders and orgasms.

There are so many Toms that it doesn't matter what they sell. Their wives know that their commission is elated sexual intercourse. Success goes to Tom's penis, and its ups and downs are as mercurial as the stock market. Tom feels bullish and bearish when he has successfully made what he calls "a killing." Their sexual life is proportionately related to his successful sales spiels.

Her secret fear: That Tom may have a bad year or—and here the mind boggles—he may lose his position as number one man with the company. The slump he will fall into should that happen will leave her physically exhausted. For the only time he is more passionate than after a big sale is after a big loss. At that time he desperately tries to prove he is still the number one man—in bed.

Case 3: The Peeper

Egbert is a voyeur. He is always looking for the peak experience. Egbert is very much the spectator in the sex act. He is so concerned with whether or not he is arousing his wife to a sufficient peak, that he is constantly staring into her face for signs of passion while they engage in sex. Since sex is supposed to be the Adult Spontaneous Spectator Sport, Egbert feels that he is supreme when he plays the spectator and the performer at the same time.

Hannah has learned to play the game with him and now they both watch each other watching each other. They have passed several tests which knocked other players out of the game. Orgasms hadn't come too easily to Hannah at first, but she earned some laurels when she had multiple orgasms last Spring. Two weeks ago she was able to achieve two clitoral orgasms and one vaginal orgasm during one session. She knew by the expression on Egbert's face that she had pleased him. They are working on the big M now—the Mutual Climax.

Her secret dream: One day they will lie in each other's arms and hold each other tenderly and do nothing else but feel close. He will whisper softly to her and tell her how much he loves her.

Her secret fear: One day Egbert will accuse her of not watching at a crucial moment. She may not watch because she's getting sleepier and sleepier from having watched this performance so many times before.

Case 4: The Dildo Dodo

Don is a Dildo Dodo. He responds to all the mail order ads which advertise dildoes, vibrators, clitoral-ticklers, penis-stretchers and anything new which he can experiment with. His theory is simple: why not try to give his wife as much pleasure as he can? When he can't, he simply finds something which can substitute for him. His wife has talked to her friends. They aren't quite at the point where Don is. They have just reached the XXX Blue Movies Stage with their husbands, which was the stage which followed the hard core erotic literature.

While most people recognize that any erotic stimulation is fine between a couple as long as they enjoy it and don't impose it on others, Don is much past that stage. He has a fetish for the sexy substitute and has no idea that his own warmth and softness is really what his wife is looking for. He rarely enjoys "simple sex," for to him the object of his affection is all too often an object he bought in a store. His wife Sarah knows that these substitutes stimulate him, because the more extreme the position, the more exotic the substitute, the more aroused he gets just thinking about how he must be exciting her.

Her Secret Fear: She is wondering when he'll suggest the ultimate: a large group orgy all wired together so that each man's motions will start a chain of orgasms which never stop.

Case 5: The Faker Maker

Filbert is a faker maker. He has made Fanny fake her orgasms for years. But Filbert doesn't know that his wife is a true artist at pretending to reach consummate bliss during intercourse. Her act of deception is matched only by the ingenuity of her husband to determine if she is faking or not.

It all began when her ardor would die after repeated attempts on his part to continue stimulating her to more and greater orgasms. She finally gave up her right to total sex satisfaction and settled for satisfying her partner by faking. She doesn't mind. She always has one mild but pleasant orgasm which is sufficient for her. She is somewhat proud at times of how authentic her orgasms appear.

Filbert and Fanny are intrepid players in this game. Both are undaunted although sometimes they suspect that they both know what is happening.

Her secret fear: that the whole thing is an exercise in futility. For both will lose points if her deception is detected. Sometimes she feels she should tell him what she is doing. But she just can't bring herself to do it. She'd hate to have him feel that he couldn't trust her.

This chapter has been devoted to the man known as the Sexual Athlete. The birth of the Sex Athlete may be seen as an interesting outgrowth of centuries of sexual insanity. His presence in modern society and our ability to recognize him, admit his existence, takes on immense importance. For unless he can understand why he behaves the way he does, why competition and performance hold such high priorities in his life, he will never be able to reprogram himself. And reprogram himself he must, if he is to ever have the honest, warm and close relationships which man and woman can achieve both in their sexual relations and in all human contacts. He has to know himself, and be aware of himself before he can move towards intimacy. Otherwise, he will remain a sexual robot, constantly subjected to the forces of the Manipulator, the Collector and the Brat in sexual interactions.

Retraining the Sexual Athlete

What are you doing over there, Lady?

What are you doing over there, Sir?

Well, there is this damned bridge.
Between us.
How do I reach you?

Just cross the bridge—
The Intimacy Bridge

But there are things on this side.
I have to do a few things
Before I can cross.

Come on over. It's worth it.

Okay, Ready or not,
Here I come.

I'm ready, Sir.
Believe me, I'm ready.
Do you have any idea?

Idea of what?

Of how long I've been waiting?

Chapter 5

Retraining The Sexual Athlete

Society, the Master Dealer, the Man with The Golden Arm, deals out the punch cards which programmed the male to emerge as the non-intimate man. We took a close look at that man in the form of the Sexual Athlete. If he re-programs himself, retrains himself, turns the tape back and rewinds the reel, he can start off into a different and much more desirable direction: true intimacy with a woman.

The Sexual Athlete is a component of all men. He resides to a huge degree in some, and to a much lesser degree in others. How much of him exists in a man is going to directly influence the intimacy he can enjoy with a woman. We know how he came to be; how he emerged as a symbol of sexual prowess and sexual competition. To reprogram him, or perhaps just the parts of him that are so destructive to any true intimacy, let's look at the essentials for an honest, loving relationship with a woman. There are things we men have to know about ourselves; there are truths we have to understand about women.

Remember the little verse which many a young man and woman used to be titillated by? It went something like this:

"Balls," said the Queen.

"If I had those, I'd be King."

The King laughed. He had two.

The Queen cried. She wanted two.

Well, a lot of kings who are supposed to have two aren't laughing, and the Queens are saying: "Come on buddy, you've got two, and I know it. I may wish I did too, but I don't—I never will, and what's more, I got over it. When will you accept that I don't want yours?

Since his balls have been so integral to his functioning in a man-made society, and because his penis has always been a representation of his ego and his strength and what separates him from whatever girls are, the competitive and fearful elements women represent are very significant. When men react with such trepidation, a woman's face becomes both sides of a coin. Spin the coin, and the smiling face takes on a leer. He may then experience a gut-level aversion to what is spinning in front of him, laughing at him. As long as he sees it that way, such consternation provides a very successful antidote to honesty, openness, trust and intimacy. How can we turn with warmth to that which we fear?

His fears of failure, of being wrong are so enormous that they endow the woman with a power she never had or wanted. His original obsession about remaining intact disintegrates him, fragments him, splinters him. He alienates himself from women and worries that she may do things faster, with more aplomb and "savoir faire" or sophistication. In short, that she will make him look like a clod; that she will embarrass him by exposing his secret scar. At those moments the name of the game becomes Status and Image. Such status spells masculinity. It spells penis. And it spells balls, with the queen no longer whining that if she had them, she'd be king. At *that* point, he is convinced that she *has* them, convinced that she *took* them from him.

And yet, in spite of his concern about his inadequacies, men want to be close to women. They yearn for such closeness. Certainly, the women want the same kind of intimacy with men. Something interferes. What? That something, that deterrent to the happy interaction which both sexes are hungry for, is the man's constant conviction that woman is, essentially, his natural enemy. He suspects her and worries that she is going to emasculate him if she sees how inadequate he feels.

Now there is nothing new or brilliant about that concept. Freud said it first, and he said it better so many years ago: Boys fear castration. So what? Where do we go from there? Saying it, theorizing it, repeating it ad nauseum is quite ridiculous. The important question is: Isn't it about time we did something about it? Isn't it about time we took some steps to get over our incredible terror which divides the sexes into two warring camps where collaboration with the enemy has so many built-in dangers?

Women know all about our problems with our manhood fears. It's our problem, and sometimes they add to it and exaggerate it, but essentially it is always our unique and special private dilemma. A woman really can't do too much about it, other than to wait for us to stop being so terrified that she'll play the grab-the-genitals game.

I'm a man. I know the fears. I have had them too. But too often our fears of Woman debilitate us. She doesn't want to vie with us and destroy our male image, because she needs us. She needs us desperately, and she wants to be close. She can and will be our friend if we give her a chance. But we must convince her, finally, that we are willing to be friends with her, to lift the barriers, drop the smoke screens, and extend the hand of friendship. The foundation for such friendship is no different from what we seek in our male friends. Why do you like your best friend? Because he is loyal. Because you respect him. Because he is fun. Perhaps because you know he is no threat to you and likes you in return. Along the way you have probably built a storehouse of good memories and fun times with him. If you need to confide in someone and expect the same from another, it is that friend to whom you will turn.

Now, I'm suggesting that the same relationship can exist with a woman. A basic and solid foundation based on those prerequisites for friendship have to exist between a man and a woman before they can consider themselves friends. Oh yes, sprinkle in sex, and you may have a romance. Remove the sex, and hopefully, you still have a friend.

There are steps the man can take to convince the girl that he is finally ready to be friends with her. Notice the wording. He has to convince *her* that he is ready to be *her* friend. She waits, has been waiting anxiously for that day. And the day is today— now. Women have to feel that men don't dread them, or respond to them with apprehension and anxiety. If they see that men don't have to exclude women from their lives, and that men have gotten over the alienation crises, women will step forward to grasp their hands, not twist their testicles.

It means that the man has to take some very necessary steps. He has to cross some bridges which separate him from women. Remember, the androgynous man and woman were once one ball, as Plato pointed out—Unified. Today, there is a schism separating them. Those first steps are essential for ultimate intimacy between man and woman. It won't be easy, but it can be done. It will, in essence, take balls to get back our balls.

What are these bridges?

1) Accept that women know him better than he knows them.

2) Accept the female side of himself.

3) Accept the child within himself.

4) Accept the foolish, not-so-bright side of himself.

The First Bridge:

A man has to recognize, finally, that he does not know women very well. Women know men *far* better. We humans tend to fear and mistrust what we don't know or understand. Finally accepting women as equal is crucial and fundamental to a retooling of the die which was cast in the nonintimate mold during his childhood days. He simply has got to stop excluding her from what he considers his private male domain.

It's a difficult concession for man, admitting that he doesn't know women. A still greater concession is admitting that women know him far better than he knows them. Men like to *think* they know women. They brag about it quite often. Women hear them, and they know *he* shouldn't know how much *they* know. Man wants it that way; he demands such concessions from women; and in deference to his need, many women give it to him. And it's the biggest mistake they can make, as we shall see later.

A woman knows when she is a threat to a man. It is apparent to her that he does not completely trust her; she is aware that he doesn't understand her. She knows that it is questionable that he is even comfortable in her company.

Men have private dialogues going on at some subliminal level much of the time. The dialogue is complex, often relating to his huge concern that the woman will see through him and compete too successfully with him in too many areas. At those times his secret dialogue may go something like this:

I don't trust you. I'm afraid of you.

Sometimes I hope that if I close my eyes you will just disappear. But I'm more realistic than that, because I couldn't get along without you.

You are here, and you are here to stay. And you are a threat. Maybe you can do things better. Maybe you are smarter. Maybe you'll see through me for what I am, a phony, or a showoff, with muscles pasted on from a Charles Atlas "97 pound weakling" ad. Or whatever.

Don't expect me to remember all the threats you pose. It's a long list. But you're on it, baby, you're on it. I'm going to watch you and not just for your curvy body either. Even your dumbness I suspect. I never really have felt comfortable with you.

Remember the parties we'd have during our high school days? How easily we went to opposite corners of the room? We would try all kinds of games, to pair us off. Too bad. It never worked. We're still in different corners of the room watching each other. Carefully. It's not really your fault. I have to be on guard, and you wouldn't understand that. How could you? You can't feel what a man feels, can you?

Man has an investment in his manhood which woman doesn't have in her womanhood. His ego is quite intertwined with his penis and his erogeneity. When he experiences threats against those, he suffers sharp, cutting attacks against his masculinity.

Not knowing women too well, he misinterprets their motivations and their attitudes. Too often he sees an assault where none is intended. He becomes counterphobic in his defense of what he feels has been subject to scrutiny and appraisal: his virility. His biggest mistake is in assuming that she has no conception of what is male, no awareness of his fears.

He is confused enough in his interpretation of what makes a man that to him it becomes Bogart, or a trenchcoat, or Cagney pushing a grapefruit into some "smart-assed" woman's face. He really thinks that being a man embraces the whole John Wayne syndrome where he can take on the tribe—not of Apaches—but of women who are ready to scalp him by the pubic hairs. Trenchcoat-Bogart-Wayne then spell M-A-N, along with chest hair, six-packs, hardhats, and touchdowns.

The skirmish makes the adrenalin flow, and anxieties flow with them. The career-competition gargoyle raises its menacing head. He worries about not being too bright. He wonders, if, in truth, he isn't shallow. He read somewhere that dull people talk about things; average people talk about people; intelligent people talk about ideas. The intelligent woman challenges him in her quest for the Original Idea. At times he is convinced that he falls into some dirty-gray area somewhere between the dull and the average. And he doesn't want to test it out.

Women know that the phallus stands at half-mast when he is threatened, and his manhood has died. Because they need men, how to reassure him and prevent the mourning at half-mast is a chronic woman-problem. She tries to reason with him. She tries to act a little dumber than she is. She tries laughing at the jokes she knew even before she met him and has heard him tell over and over. "That's the first time I heard that joke," she'll tell him. And to herself she'll mumble, "today." She'll try to promote commonalities between them, but she constantly feels the push-pull in their relationship. His message is clear: "There are areas where you are a threat. That's when you'll be excluded. When you don't threaten, when you don't scare me, that's when I'll let you in." Too often he even excludes her from his greatest area of expertise, his career.

The one thing which should bring a man and woman closer should be the sharing of his career. It doesn't matter whether he is a plumber, an exterminator, a steamlifter, a college professor, or president of a huge industrial empire. At least it *shouldn't* matter. Here is one area where the woman can develop an ever-increasing respect for the man. It's where he lives and spends so much of his time in a world which is often quite foreign, even mystical, to his wife or girlfriend. But he still fears her criticism-questioning-advising, and finds it too easy to lock her out. And the men talk to me of their feelings:

We can't talk of my work, you know.
Why not?
She doesn't understand it.
It's too difficult for her to understand?
Yes. (Pause) Well, no, I guess she could understand it all right.
Well then?
I live with the damned thing all day. I haven't the patience to go over it with her.
But you said you can't talk of your work.
Look, let's not play with words. I don't want to talk about it.
Why not?
Well, for one thing, I have plenty of people I can talk to about it all day. I'd rather talk of other things.
I see. Like what?
Like what?
Yes. Like what?
Oh, I don't know. Anything. Politics. The children...
Do you enjoy talking about those things?
Sometimes. I guess not usually, though.
It seems your field of work is a gray area,

a kind of no-man's land.

(laughing) No. It's kind of no-woman's land.

Too bad you have to lock her out.

Yes. It is too bad. I guess I can't blame her.

Do you blame yourself?

No. It's just the way things are. You understand.

Yes. We both understand.

Sure.

Only one problem.

What's that?

The lady doesn't.

It has become so hack, so cliché, to talk about the struggling whosis who became a successful whatsis and found that he spent more and more time pursuing his whatsis career. One day he finds that he has less and less time to discuss his work, with his wife or his girlfriend. And to think he once saw her as his indispensable right arm! Huge gaps, great non-intimate areas grow rapidly. And then, one day, I talk with the woman.

He stays out later and later.

Um. Hummm.

Sometimes I wonder if...

Do you suspect him?

Oh, no. Not really. He works very hard.

Um. Hmmm.

I mean he's always been very conscien-

tious and hard working.

I see.

It's just that...

Yes?

Why the hell does he have to be so busy?

I don't know, what does he do?

He was a struggling whosis, but now he's a very successful whatsis.

Oh, I see.

I really don't know too much about his work.

Oh?

Well, I have the children, and the house, and that sort of thing, after all. You know.

Of course.

Somehow I never figured we'd grow so far apart, and I'd never share his work. It didn't start out that way.

Um. Hmmm.

That's what attracted me to him in the beginning.

What's that?

He was hard working, and I felt he would make it.

Well, he still is, and he has, hasn't he?

Yes. And I respect him for that believe me. I really do.

But?

I just thought I'd be more a part of it, of...of...

Of?

Of him.

The man, the career. So very intertwined. In our modern world, with the commune and the liberated woman and her de-emphasis on the material, and the serious questioning of the established Horatio Alger model as the final goal, the ultimate happiness, a woman still expects the man to be able to do *something* in terms of "making the bread." She'll pitch in, she'll help out, she'll "go dutch" if they are dating, and she won't weigh the career-income-security triad as heavily as her grandmother or her mother.

But career is still a factor. And it always will be. A man stands taller and straighter when he feels he is heading somewhere or has gotten there. He has a spirit and a twinkle and a bounce which show his self-satisfaction and his self-respect. Women absorb those feelings and those qualities and respect men all the more for it. She may adore him for his personality, looks, and sex appeal. But she also has to respect his ability to "make it out there" and to share his work with her. Yes, she will contribute whatever mental, moral, or physical support she can.

So why doesn't the man allow a gut-level alliance? She isn't a partner—not a senior one anyway. Often she isn't even a junior partner. Many women tell me they aren't partners at all. An incredibly large number of women don't even know how much their men earn! Why does the man exclude her, in the final analysis? He again pursues a policy of rugged individualism. His career, which could have been the cement, the meshing of the gears, as it were, between them, in reality creates greater distances.

The woman tries to understand. She tries to laugh it off. And when she can't laugh anymore, when she can no longer reason with him, she experiences a powerful frustration. Putting it simply, when rivalry, panic, threats, genitalia, six-packs, Archie Bunkeritis and "no-woman's-going-to-push-me-around" continue to spell manhood to her man, she is finally helpless and impotent to fight against such powerful imagery. In frustration she feels she must join him, and stop threatening him, or just quit the game. The consequences of forsaking him are so shattering that she checks her imaginary six-shooter at the door, walks in with palms up, wearing short sleeves so nothing can be hidden, and finally stands in front of the man, waiting for him to make the first move. She knows that if she makes any sudden moves, he may have to attack, if only in self-defense. He then may realize as she falls that she was only reaching for a cigarette or pulling out a compact to powder her nose, and there she is lying on the ground, bleeding from her wounds.

Thus, man too often obviates any invasion she can make into his private life, because he still experiences moments—even long periods of time—when he is simply not comfortable with a woman. We see the bars where the women are not allowed, or at least, not welcome. We know about the "night out with the boys" for poker or bowling. The lunch breaks with their buddies which allow them to talk freely for hours are legendary. We still see the socials and the clambakes at the Club where the men play the old high school game of "let's go to one end of the room so we can be away from the broads." And then, of course, there is always the ubiquitous TV, where he shares his beer in idyllic isolation with 22 men playing football, when he isn't out with the boys playing golf.

He locks her out of his career and his man-moments. And then he turns to her for sex. It is amazing how many men don't realize that women can't enjoy sex unless they can feel a spiritual and emotional attachment to the sex partner. She simply has to have that spiritual content in the sex act or it has little meaning for her. She has been forced to look at him through a glass wall which he erected and which separates them, and then, suddenly, they are supposed to enjoy mutual intimacy in their sexual embraces. Unaware of her needs, he expects her to be prepared to join him, be his partner, be his confidante, be his associate, be his friend, be his lover, and feel she is an integral part of his life.

It doesn't work that way. If he knew women a little better he would know that. The glass wall allows them to see each other, but for her that isn't enough. He is caught in the quagmire of early conditioning, for he learned to set up that glass wall as a youth, when he would jump over from time to time for sex, or sex-stimulation, and then slip back to his male-haven.

As long as the man continues to feel "different" from women, he will keep alive the spirit of the Sexual Athlete. He makes the girl a competitor to be wary of on the one hand, and a desirable sex object to chase, manipulate, and ultimately conquer on the other. With Veni, Vidi, Vici—I came, I saw, I conquered—the Sex Athlete learns to flex his muscles.

If the man continues to see a unidimensional kind of relationship with a woman which calls for occasional conversation between orgasms, he may succeed in sporadic bursts of sexual closeness with her. She is very capable of enjoying that physical involvement, those lovely embraces. But to confuse that with total intimacy is to ignore the three sides of a triangle. Physical intimacy is but one of the three sides. There are, after all, two other dimensions—emotional and intellectual intimacy.

If a man is going to be honest with himself; if he is going to make a genuine attempt to get along with women, he has to arrive at an understanding of *why* he excludes women so often from his life. Is it because he is still uncomfortable with them? Still aware of their threats to him? In that case, he can never understand them any better than he could a male friend with whom he too often felt uncomfortable and spent time with on some sporadic basis because he "had to." That friend could never truly be a friend. We all know people we see infrequently but who are still our dearest friends. That's because we truly enjoy their company but our lifestyles keep us apart—not discomfort with each other.

If a man's relationship with a girl is a healthy one, his life style certainly makes allowances for his night out, his poker, his bowling, his whatever. That's simply adding new and different dimensions to his life. He isn't avoiding relating to the girl for the wrong reasons. Only you, as a man, can know the answer, then, to the fundamental question: Do you exclude the female from your life because she makes you uncomfortable? Or are you so comfortable with her that those other activities are not retreats, escapes, but a part of a relationship which allows for "time out from each other?"

One bridge to be crossed: admitting that the woman knows man better than he knows her. If a man can accept that first one, he will be prepared to cross the second bridge too; accepting the female with himself.

*The Second Bridge:
Accepting the Female in Himself*

A man has to be willing to accept the female in himself and not deny or exclude it from his life. To do that he has to make a concession: stop fighting this tender, gentle side of himself, and let go of the Superman concept which says "I am *all* man, and I'll punch anyone in the nose who suggests otherwise."

When I was a boy I was often called "Stark" or "Starkey." I considered it quite natural, and I would respond—or perhaps the word is retaliate—by calling others in my classes or my neighborhood by their last names too. The point is that it was reserved for boys, this last-name calling. I don't recall girls at the elementary school level calling other girls by their last names. It was a curiously intimate thing between boys; a male anomaly. With early queueing up on the line which read "for boys only," the boundaries were being drawn and the ground rules of the boy-girl divisive rituals were being established.

Parents often allow for and even extend this separation of the sexes. They widen the breech, for example, by their frequent willingness to endow their girl-child with names which are extensions of masculinity. Thus we get Roberta, and Paula, and Edwina. Do parents feel they unconsciously attach some strength to the girl through such masculinizing? Is it her place card on the smorgasbord table which says the goodies in life are for the man in a man's world? Do they feel that the suggestion of maleness overcomes the disadvantages of a name like Violet or Rose? By calling the girl Roberta, she may well be called Bobby later in life. In the same vein, many girls are called "Chris," and "Sandy," and "Pat." It just seems desirable, apparently to aim towards maleness—even through osmosis.

It never quite works out the same way, however, with boys. Many a young man with a strange-sounding name has had a difficult childhood and was laughed at by boys and girls alike. A recent study revealed that boys with funny-sounding first names even did poorly in school, partly from their own poor achievements, and incredibly enough, because the teachers appeared to be negatively biased towards them! The separation of the male from the female begins early if a sexual hierarchy exists in the very selection of the infant's name.

A few years back a very funny song was entitled: "A Boy Named Sue." What made it funny was that Sue was a man. A deep baritone voice would sing:

My name is Sue
How do you do?

Apparently Sue went through life, in the song, fighting for his manhood with a quick left hook and a quick draw. His one goal in life was to find his father—the one who named him Sue—and kill him. At the end of the song he does finally catch up with his father and does try to kill him. A wild fight follows, and we learn that the father who had deserted the family, named the infant Sue in the hopes that such a hardship would make him stronger and better able to face problems. The reasoning may have been spurious, but it certainly was practical.

To invest the male with female qualities in this very male world, is apparently seen as a huge burden to carry. From the start the boy-child is very concerned with preserving that maleness, and in telling the world that he has exorcised any femaleness out of him. He fears that Inquisition of his peers, and seems to need to prove he is purified and without the dreaded womanly qualities. Hobbies, interests, desires, and vocations which smack of femininity, and sometimes even artistry, are too often suspect if they are pursued by the male. Knowing this, the young man too often has to "go underground," and pursue his interests in secrecy.

We have posited that a man must accept the female who resides within him. We keep talking about a "man." What is a man? It's easier to answer that question by first suggesting what manhood is *not*. It is *not* beating one's chest. It is *not* walking around swaggering, developing muscles and painting tattoos. It is *not* cursing and roaring when upset. It is *not* the rugged individualist who never cries, never knows fear, never turns to others for help. Such a total M-A-N becomes a caricature, a monstrous exaggeration and a composite of the quiet Man, the Hairy Ape, and Philip Marlow looking for the Maltese Falcon.

What then is a real man? The real man is gentle, and tender and unafraid to show that side of himself. He is frightened at times. He worries and he admits it. He is timid at times and quite confused, and unafraid of it. He even fails at many things he feels are important. And he can admit that too. For our real man can take the chance of being humble. Humility includes accepting that gentle side which is the vestigial female trace within him. He can be humble because he is secure enough to acknowledge tht female side. The real man then, knows that the quiet female residing in him has found a home and is accepted.

I took time out from my writing today to read a Long Island newspaper, *Newsday*. A major feature story concerned itself with the bombing by terrorists of an Athens airport. Many were injured, and three were killed. A special feature described the relatives waiting at the Kennedy Airport for the return of their loved ones after the horrible ordeal.

In another part of the lounge Mr. and Mrs. Blank Blank of Such and such place waited for their 14-year-old daughter... They had driven down from a vacation house in Maine. Mr. Blank Blank had never cried openly in front of his wife. Yesterday, he wept openly.

How fantastic! Married all those years and yet he had never felt the need, never experienced the luxury of weeping in front of his wife. The reporter considered that important enough to include it in the story. Mr. Blank Blank was finally able to let his wife in on his secret—he cries, he bleeds, he worries. Now, of course, his wife knows. Will he ever be able to do it again, or will it take another tragedy for him to muster up enough anti-male behavior to cry again sometime in the future?

The non-intimate man, by not accepting

the female in himself, becomes too easily confused and frightened when tenderness and gentleness are expected or demanded of him. He masks such feelings, and denies them and ultimately he succeeds in repressing them. Since he considers women silly, hysterical, illogical, and erratic, why on earth would he want to allow any such qualities to emerge from him?

Female: How do you feel about women?

Male: They're lovely.

Female: Yes, but how do you feel about them?

Male: Wouldn't want a world without them.

Female: Yes, but how do you feel about them?

Male: You mean sex? (*His smile has gone. There is irritation in his voice now.*) How do I feel about them? Like what?

Female: Well, like emotionally.

Male: Oh, I guess they are a little more emotional than men. You know, they get hysterical easier and things like that. Not much good in an emergency. Things like that, you know.

Female: Men are more stable and handle problems better...

Male: (*Rolling his eyes upwards in exasperation*) I don't know if you're putting me on or not.

Female: No, I'm serious.

Male: Well, of course they are. Women are a little—er.

Female: It's okay. You can say it.

Male: All right. A little silly. Giggly. (*Exasperated*) What the hell, lady, they're dizzy.

Female: You mean women aren't mannish. Manly.

Male: That's right. That's it.

Female: They laugh easier and cry more and fall apart easier. Things like that?

Male: That's it. A large part of it. At a party you can hear them screeching. They screech when they laugh, and they make all those high-pitched female sounds.

Female: Men don't do that so often, do they?

Male: Not the men *I* know. Not the ones

I associate with. Believe me, I don't mix with pansies, lady.

Female: A real man wouldn't do anything like those softies, would he?

Male: Hell, no. No man wants to make a jackass out of himself.

Female: I didn't think women did, either.

Male: Did what?

Female: Want to make jackasses out of themselves.

Male: (*Laughing with a guffaw but definitely not a high screech*). That's great. You have a great sense of humor. But you just proved my point.

Female: How's that?

Male: (*Still chuckling*). Females can't... (*bursts into laughter again*) be jackasses can they? That's a male animal.

Female: (*smiling*) Yes. I guess that's true.

That scene was a burlesque. It was jest. But the essence of burlesque is to take the everyday foibles of life and exaggerate them to the ludicrous until penetrating truths emerge. At that point we laugh. If we have a true sense of humor we may even laugh at ourselves. But that scene was not as funny as it could have been because the total rejection of the female by the male, the need to preserve his manhood at all costs, made him an easy victim to the whiplashes of his own fears. To such men, men and women are divided into unreal warring camps, where truces on holidays and special occasions take place. It's a war where the most perilous offense too often is collaboration with the enemy.

A man has two options open to him; to accept the female within him, or to refuse to acknowledge that part of himself. It's a kind of crossroads which every man has to face.

If he accepts the female in him, then he accepts *her*. Her presence within him does not haunt him, torment him, or create a violent anti-body within him which he must worry about destroying. In accepting her he allows himself to accept her qualities; tender, soft, gentle, irrational, foolish, giggly, illogical, and all the myriad adjectives men like to ascribe to the female. Muscles and brawn cease being a problem. She is from man; he is from woman. They are one. He takes her in, and reveals himself to her as he accepts her. Such unity is a true merger. It's a forerunner to the final, ultimate intimacy. With that acceptance he moves closer to the woman's outstretched hand, and is ready to cross the Third Bridge.

The Third Bridge:
Accepting the Child Within

A man has to learn to accept the child in himself. It is there, smiling in its innocence. The concession: Don't just accept the child in us all; expose him to the world around you. The man who will have trouble establishing intimacy with a woman is the man who fears she will lose respect for him if she sees this delightful child-like part.

The man was once a boy. What a simple observation! The man-boy, of course, is still both. But he is so afraid of that child in him that he keeps him submerged. I am stressing here that an essential for intimacy with a woman, then, is to revive the child in the man. Too often he holds the child in him behind his back, like a bouquet of flowers he wants to present but won't because he fears looking foolish. When does he expose the child? Mostly with other men. That's why he is so comfortable with men in locker rooms and any other female-excluded settings.

The man who can be a child has a curious charm for women, assuming that she has built up at least a modicum of respect for him. But first, let us understand what a child is, and what he is not. A child's nose runs; he drops food down from the sides of his mouth when he eats; he whines when he does not get what he wants, and he bursts into tears if it rains when he was supposed to pitch in the Little League on Sunday. To pursue that child image is as silly as the pursuit of the man-image cursing and beating his hairy chest. There is another child in all men. The open, ingenuous, naive, wide-eyed and ready-to-learn child. That child is spontaneous in laughter, with the ability to swing from being fantasy-filled and imaginative, to being very reality-based. There is the child in all of us who is ready to expose himself; to joke, laugh and be unafraid to take chances. We have to resurrect him. He's never really been dead. He's always there. And he's a delightful, funny, lovable and loving part of us all who doesn't have to make his debut only when we are drugged with the spirits of whiskey or euphoria.

Women respond to that child. They respond to the bumbling of Woody Allen. The wide-eyed ingenuousness of Montgomery Clift is appealing to them. The boyishness and naughty glint-in-the-eye of Robert Redford and Paul Newman—short of any trace of the macho—is seductive and desireable to the female.

Such figures offer the promise of being

occasionally able to excite their fantasies. The most exciting people I know are fantasy-filled, and fun-filled. That person gets close to a woman, or anyone else for that matter.

I have tried it. At first I found it strange to reconcile any looseness and flexibility with my image and status of Doctor. But now it's part of me. I tell people: "I'll tell you my fantasies and show my child side. Join me if you want. I think you'll like it." And, when they do join, they *do* enjoy, and we both like it.

It's fun to be naive; to ask the question that has to be asked just because you don't know the answer. Suddenly you find you're asking the questions everyone else wanted to ask. What a fantastic feeling! You broke the ground, you took the plunge, and then everyone is diving into the pool with you. My naive questions can easily be dum-dum questions. At times it makes me seem immature, and people look a little shocked. What did they expect? A Van Dyke Beard, a heavy pair of horn-rimmed glasses and a thick Viennese accent? That's not me. I can't live up to some predetermined character actor's part the world wants to assign to me. Teenagers know that when you do that what results is a "tightass." What emerges is a lock-step kind of approach to life: logic-tight compartments which suffocate one, and make life complicated and unpleasant. It's but a short step from allowing the child in us to come out, to completing the quadrangle necessary for intimacy.

The Fourth and Last Bridge:
A Man Must be Ready to Accept the Foolish, Not-Too-Bright Side of Himself

A man has finally to accept, difficult as it may be, the not-so-brilliant, the inadequate, and the unknowing side of himself, and not be afraid to expose that to the female. I have said this before, but it is important to repeat it here.

I have found that most people fear two things: that they are secretly quite stupid and that they are secretly quite crazy.

I found it terribly difficult the first time I did something which might confirm in people's eyes my own fears of being odd, different. I talked to a stranger; I smiled and blinked my eyes in Morse Code at a wide-eyed child; I touched a casual acquaintance on the cheek as I talked. I took a chance. Try it sometime. The sky doesn't fall down! Take more chances. Try once in a while doing the opposite of what you have been taught. Fight the sameness your tapes demand. You have long since rejected much of what you once considered sacred in your early teachings. Why follow them so desperately? Start out by admitting your ignorance in an area and your lack of knowledge even in your own skill-career-profession. It's wonderful to be able to admit your stupidity and inadequacy and get away with it. And watch people dive into that pool with you. Didn't Socrates say "I know only one thing—and that is that I know nothing"?

This fourth step is probably the hardest one. It's easy for the child to master, for there is so much for him to learn and absorb in such a wide range of areas, and we tolerate, even encourage, his asking us questions. What makes the picture show on the TV screen? Why can birds stand on a high-voltage wire and not get electrocuted? What makes an itch itch, and why does scratching make it stop itching? I don't know the answer to those questions. I don't even know why I had a headache yesterday. If you and I ever meet, and I feel for one minute you might have the answer to that question or one of 50 I'd love to ask, you can be sure of one thing: I'll ask. Will I look naive? Childish? Dumb? Maybe. But is your act that of the austere adult? I have gone through life asking the most amazing questions and exposing the most childlike qualities I possess. And only one thing has ever happened: If people feel I am sincere and not putting them on, they will try to answer if they can. And they may not have the answer at all. It really doesn't matter. By the time we've gone through the issue, we are closer for it. If I keep those questions and that side of me to myself, I deny that child-like curiosity, and I never learn. What's more, I never expose myself to people. And I can never get close. Does the answer to the question really matter? Even if neither of us knows the answer, what fun we'll have taking a little journey into Wonderland together!

A few years ago I was dining with my American friends in a restaurant in London. I remembered a word I'd read somewhere: bumbershoot. I thought it might be an umbrella which English men carry with them when they wear their cute derbies which they call "bowlers." I asked the waiter what a "bumbershoot" was. He screwed his face up, frowned deeply and said he had never heard of it. Some people nearby chuckled. The waiter looked at me strangely. But he was a gentleman, or had I aroused his curiosity also? He called over the Maitre D'. Same reaction: "bumbershoot?" "Never heard of it. That's not an English word, sir." But something had been stirred, and some kind of electricity started a current in the room. People were diving in and finding the water was just great. Diners at tables nearby started whispering among themselves, and finally, chuckling. One leaned over, and with a warm smile informed me there was no such word. At this point it didn't really matter. At this point it never does. The closeness from the naiveté, and the openness and the childlike honesty brings an intimacy with it. And that makes it worth while. Finally the manager came over, and he too laughingly but respectfully assured me there was no such word.

In the lobby my group chatted with two English couples. "By the way," I asked, "what's a bumbershoot?" Incredibly the four of them began to argue among themselves, and then they decided I was just confused and that I must have "bamboo shoots" or some Italian word in mind. Laughing as we left the restaurant, they waved and said "Good luck with your bumbershoot, Yank."

For the rest of my stay in England, in shops in Soho, in theaters, in taxis, I asked what a bumbershoot was. I amused them. They laughed. They were compassionate. But they never knew.

Back in America, I forgot the whole incident. One night, I looked in the dictionary for the meaning of another word and decided, just for the fun of it, to look up "bumbershoot." And there it was. What was a bumbershoot? Why it *was* an umbrella which English men carried with them when they wore their cute derbies they call "bowlers!"

I don't understand it. And it doesn't really matter. But I enjoyed England just a little more, for during my blundering for the "bumbershoot" I was able to laugh and feel close—even intimate—with strangers who responded to a little innocence in what is too often a skeptical world. I have a feeling a number of Londoners chuckle in the pub when they recall that funny American with his silly questions. I think they enjoyed him. I *know* he enjoyed them.

Again, try it sometime. You're just like me. You get sudden and spontaneous urges to do things which aren't always totally adult. If it isn't too immoral, illegal, or indecent, why don't you do it? Or say it? Bury that quality in you, and you suffocate man-woman relationships in particular, and closeness in general.

I have fun with my childishness. It's fun to be a little dumb, a little stupid. All kinds of walls and all kinds of insulation drop away. If you work at it, you can allow your inadequacies to show, the child to show. Above all, you can do it with a woman, who understands and is hungry for it. Women love to see that tender, gentle side exposed. And it *doesn't* bring about what men fear so desperately; loss of respect and loss of a "mannish" feeling in the eyes of the woman. Women find such men interesting and exciting and alive. Women love children, and they love the child-adult.

Conclusion:

So there it is. I know that I have been hard, sometimes brutally so, on the man. But never, I feel, unfairly. Men have lived too long with their fears and have built up too many cults based on a phallic divinity which on the one hand was seen as sacrosanct, but on the other hand was coveted with a devotion based on incredible panic and fear. It's time we destroyed the cult and exposed it for what it is, a false sense of security and a dedication to a virtual hierarchy of the sexes. It has always been a philosophy promulgated by false prophets. It's time we recognize the existence of the iron jock strap as something as ludicrous and anachronistic as the chastity belt.

In this chapter we looked at the four bridges a man has to cross to reach intimacy with a woman. A man must finally recognize if he has never known intimacy. He may have known the exhilaration of the conquest, the groan of the orgasm, the power of the pelvic thrust. He has known scoring and performance and closeness of bodies. But he may never have known real closeness. He has thrilled women, excited women, elevated them to orgiastic heights—even made them feel lovely and desirable many times. But he has also conquered women, browbeaten women, hoodwinked women and scoffed at them with a patronizing and placating air. He too often never really understood that the women saw through it all, and recognized that they were the quarry, he was the hunter and the bed was the trophy.

Men who hesitate at the bridges, who find the concessions intolerable, will remain frightened and intimidated. Such men will continue projecting all kinds of negative qualities on the woman, thinking she is frightened and intimidated. But, mister, the woman *knows* you. She knows you and understands you, and she tolerates you and the unintimate parts of you that reside in so many men. She feels she has to accept those "male" qualities because the stakes are, after all, very high for her, too. But don't—not for one minute—ever feel that you have won a victory she didn't allow you to win.

It's like crutches. When you have leaned on them for a long time, how can you put them down, throw them away without fear of falling? Yet, people throw crutches away all the time. And people learn to walk.

Again,

Accept the fact that women know you better than you know them.

Accept the female side of you.
Accept the child who is within you.
Accept the foolish, not-so-bright side of you.

The intimate men who read this chapter will not be intimidated by the four conditions. They can identify and feel an affinity with the concessions that have to be made for intimacy with a woman. Why? Because the conditions, the concessions—call them what you may—do not threaten them. When a man feels that such four-point behavior on his part will make him look weak and sissyish in the eyes of a woman, or before other men, he is terribly confused. And it is a *critical* confusion. Actually, he would reject those four points only if he worried about sharing his experiences with women, not just with men. Such worry is tantamount to handing the woman a sword, a terrible weapon which she can hold over him. To worry about being emasculated is to give the woman incredible power. Remember, the woman knows the frightened man. She looks into his eyes and reads the fear there. She sees through his bravado and recognizes his swagger for what it is; a feeble cover-up for his inadequacies, and a weak attempt at warding off the cut, the slice.

Women will know when they look into a true man's eyes that they see the eyes of a compassionate, unthreatened man. Without his defensiveness, he takes away their weapon, their power, and meets them on equal terms. In essence, if he can accept the four ways of behavior outlined in this chapter, he shows the woman he is fearless. He takes away her edge. He no longer plays the game with a handicap.

The most famous golfer in the world is practicing one day, when a sudden summer storm breaks out. Everyone runs back to the clubhouse. But he still wants to play. He runs under a tree to wait for the rain to stop. A short, thin, quiet man is also waiting under the tree.

The rain stops. The stranger asks the champion if he would like to play a round. "Sure," says the world's foremost golfer. "But I'd better give you a handicap."

"No handicap," says the stranger. "I insist," says the champ. "All right. Give me a handicap of three gotchas," says the quiet stranger. Not having the faintest idea what a "gotcha" is, the champ shrugs and agrees. They tee off on the first hole. The stranger hits a magnificent drive. The champ steps up, starts to swing, and the stranger suddenly darts in, grabs him firmly by the testicles and shouts, "gotcha!" They return to the clubhouse. The other members are there and ask the champ how he did. He

tells them: "123." The stranger? "78".

The other members are dumbfounded—flabbergasted. "123"? What kind of score is that? How come? The champ looks them straight in the eye, and in a deadly serious voice asks: "Have you ever played 17 holes waiting for the second "gotcha"?

Man's handicap then, as far as women are concerned, is the "gotcha." And it's a handicap the woman never even wanted. The Queen long ago said "you have two and I don't want them or need them." But he insisted on giving her a sword anyway. What a terrible spot she is in. She has been handed power she neither wants, knows what to do with, or is prepared to cope with in spite of her need for and readiness for a mature relationship. What does she do with the weapon his fears offer her? How does she handle it? Will she be kind? Will she become power-hungry? What courses of action are open to her?

Woman:
The Big "F" and The Ball Breaker

Let's have a race
Oh, you can beat me.
Let's race anyway.
Wow, I left you way behind.
See, I'm fantastic.

(Doesn't he know I let him win?)

Let's have a race.
You'd better not beat me.
I wouldn't dare, sweetheart.
On second thought, let's not race.
You're too much for me.

(And don't you forget it, mister.)

Let's have a race.
All right. Who will win?
I don't know. Does it matter?

It always did up to now.
In other races.

(Why don't we just make love instead?)

Chapter 6

The Big "F"

I have always contended that women are more mature and ready for intimacy than men. Because a woman is more prepared for such intimacy, she does what any human being will do when consciously or unconsciously seeking something: she will give out signals that she seeks closeness. The signals may be overt and obvious on a conscious level as an aggressive and lovely female might display, or they may be covert and subliminal such as a shy and passive woman emits. But the signals are constantly being sent out. The signs of her preparedness for maturity show up in the very early years of development.

In kindergarten the differences in maturity between the sexes rapidly emerge.

Through the elementary grades we see a peculiar phenomenon: boys have more emotional problems and are placed more often in classes and schools for the disturbed; boys have more reading problems which any remedial reading teacher will confirm; boys have more speech problems which any speech therapist well knows. Girls reach physical maturity faster and certainly we all know that a senior high school girl at the prom often looks positively maternal when she stands next to her young man, who frequently looks like a little boy in comparison. These differences appear to "flatten out" scholastically in the later years as the boys begin to become more career conscious and start directing themselves towards their goals. But essentially, the female remains more socially and emotionally mature.

In my experience as a psychoanalyst, I soon became aware that a too-large proportion of my patients were women. At the outset of my career, having completed neither enough personal analysis or living experience, I was quite prepared to expect more problemed women than men. Somehow it fit what I had always believed: Women were more hysterical, more quick to panic, more apt to see huge problems where none existed. And why shouldn't I feel that way in my late twenties and early thirties? After all, wasn't I a man?

But as time progressed, I found myself becoming more and more uneasy. Somehow, something was wrong. The women I was seeing were just not fitting the contour and the mold physically, spiritually or culturally that would support my initial breezy acceptance of their coming for help. To compound my confusion they didn't fall into any intellectual void either, so that I found myself listening to their angry outpourings with a new sense of respect. After twenty years as an analyst I am still listening but what I have heard has affected me profoundly both as man and doctor.

Yes, women *still* dominate the larger portion of my practice. My colleagues all confirm that this happens in their practices too. But if we ask *why* this is so, today we come up with some rather startling reasons.

The reason women tend to come for help more frequently is because they *will*, and the man *won't*. They are quick to see where a marriage may be sagging, or where a child may need treatment. In their interfamilial relationships they experience the same disillusionments and disappointments and frustrations. But unlike the man they are quicker to admit it, face it, oftentimes recognize where the problem lies, and most importantly, seek outside help.

Most of the men I see tend to come in,

initially, under protest. After considerable pleading, cajoling and even threatening, the woman convinces the man that it could be, after all, safe enough and not too frightening to sit down with someone else and talk out one's problems. Before he comes in the dialogue between them sounds like this:

He: What's the matter?

She: Why?

He: You don't seem like yourself. You're always nervous and jumpy these days.

She: I'm sorry, John.

He: Well, what's the matter with you? You're no fun at all these days.

She: John, I'm depressed. I'm very unhappy.

He: Well, go see a doctor. Maybe it has something to do with your periods.

She: John, I do feel a little different and grouchy at those times, but I can tell the difference. It's more than that. I think it's us. Something is wrong.

He: There you go again. Always complaining, always bitching.

She: John, I asked you so many times to talk with me. Why don't you come with me and maybe we can see what's wrong?

He: Nothing is wrong. Just stop looking for trouble and stop feeling sorry for yourself.

After a few fruitless conversations like this, Mary decides to come in, and Dr. Stark has a new female patient. Many times she has to come in over John's objections and doesn't even tell him she's finally started treatment. When I recommend that John should see somebody also, she invariably shakes her head and says he absolutely will not see anyone. And I am not surprised. It has happened so often before: this male reaction to talking one's problems over and equating it with weakness or even "sissyishness." I may then urge her to confront him, to tell him she is coming in.

She: John, you told me a while ago to see a doctor.

He: Um. Hmmm.

She: Well, I have been seeing a doctor. A Doctor Stark.

He: Good. Did he find out what's wrong

She: with you? Did he give you any medicine?

She: He's not that kind of doctor, John.

He: What do you mean?

She: He's a psychoanalyst.

He: Oh, shit!

She: He feels you should speak with someone also.

He: In a pig's eye. I don't have any problems, and I don't need a shrink.

She: Look, John...

He: Look, if you want to indulge yourself and see a shrink, go ahead. But leave me alone. I can handle my own problems, not like...

She: Not like a woman?

He: You said it, not me.

(Another variation on this dialogue would have John warning her never to go back there again because he can't afford it or just doesn't want her going. The warning often accompanies the threat that if she goes ahead with this "nutty stuff" their relationship is finished.)

In time John will probably see someone.

But when he *does* go, he will often go in a spirit of anger, feeling coerced, pulled in. Many times he starts treatment to get his "licks in," because he resents another man being his wife's or girlfriend's confidant. Sometimes he goes to "get back" at her for what he is sure are sessions in which he is being maligned. At that point the spirit of therapy is distorted into an adversary system instead of an honest opening up of problems to be explored.

It should be pointed out that once a man settles into the process of analysis, and overcomes his basic distrust of it, he usually becomes an imaginative, honest and astute patient to work with. In order to do that he has to overcome the image-threats which serve as barriers to his progress.

The previous dialogue referred to a personal problem between John and Mary. It could just as well have reflected disagreement between parents in bringing a child into therapy.

Having been a consultant to school districts for years, I soon found that women are as quick to explore their child's problems as they are to explore any other aspect of their family life. Again, in an effort to stabilize a shaky family situation, it is the woman who will go to the teacher first (and not because the man is working and claims he doesn't have time. That's too often simply a cop-out on his part). And it is the woman, the mother, who will be quicker to accept that little Johnny needs help. It is also the single girl who recognizes that her big Johnny needs help and that maybe they both should seek pre-marital counseling. Woman is consistent: she seeks help for herself where the man so often refuses; she'll go for help in solving her problems of relating to her loved ones where once again the man will be quite resistant. Teachers have told me—indeed, I have been present at many, many such conferences—that the difficult one to "convince" is the father. Many times, when the father was scheduled for a conference, the teacher has asked me to be present, expecting a difficult session. In essence the women have often searched for help; the man often sought excuses and rationalizations for little Johnny's condition.

I once asked a group of men how they would feel if each one was alone in a room filled with women. You could see them recoil, you could sense their discomfort at the thought of such an experience. The same question put to a group of women was quite revealing. Each one in the group found the prospect provocative, challenging, and, as one woman put it, "probably an interesting experience." The sexes, it would seem, are not equally comfortable with each other. Repeatedly, women tell me they enjoy men's company, enjoy talking with them—even find such company preferable to being with women. The male reaction is, at the very least, a negative one.

Nevertheless, in spite of their preference for "male conversation," another strength which women have impressed me with is their ability to get down to the "nitty gritty" with other women. At first I would hear it in the office where it was told in a humorous way: "You should hear the way we woman talk. It's funny, we tell the dirtiest jokes and talk of the most intimate things. About sex. About our children. Of our feelings about our husbands." I questioned a number of women I knew. I discovered that such talk was an index of straightforwardness and honest truth-seeking. And it appeared once again to separate the women from the men in the quest for, and realization of, intimacy. Women, it seems, *talk*. I mean, *really* talk. Not baseball and football and what men like to think of as man-talk. They talk of problems and emotional trauma they face in their everyday lives. They aren't into ego-building conversations such as men engage in which stress their sexual conquests past and present and their fantasies of further sex-career explorations. In essence, the man was too often talking about gutless, inconsequential and non-intimate small talk.

Have you ever listened to women as they sit around talking? On a park bench as the children played on the grass? Or during a coffee klatch? They are amused and amusing in turns as they speak of their most intimate life-moments with friends, children, families.

Ever watch men as they sit around talking? Or, ever watch men playing poker? It's another world, a world of deadly serious combat entered into with as little talk as possible. Quite a contrast from the girls' card games where they talk more than they play! In the man's card game, the smoke fills the room, the chips click quietly, an occasional angry burst comes from one or the other as he finds his cards are not strong enough to take in the pot. Each man sees himself as the Mississippi Gambler, a smooth, knowledgeable savant at the card table. Truly, it's winner take all. All the way, buddy, all the way. Nobody would dare talk of the weather at such a game, no less about his wife and his problems with her.

Even sexually, women want intimacy and closeness which borders on the spiritual. Many of them can't enjoy sex on a purely biological level, as so many men can. Since many men don't know this, the woman often remains an engima to him from the time he is a youth until the day he dies. He too often approaches sex relations with an eye towards sex release rather than with closeness the ultimate aim. Women, needing a spiritual feeling, seeking closeness even if they have to fake it, will ask the man to say he loves them. Just to hear it. It makes going to bed a lot easier for them. Even if they don't really believe it, they ask him to say it.

Hearing the words elevates the sexual experience beyond the biological and lends an air—sometimes camouflaged—of intimacy to the embrace. The song *"But Do You Love Me?"* from Fiddler on the Roof has universal meaning to women. To paraphrase it in a modern sex scene it would sound something like this:

He: Oh, honey. This feels so good.

She: But do you love me?

He: Mmm. You make me so hot.

She: But do you love me?

He: Oh wow baby. I just look at that body of yours, and I'm ready. You're beautiful...

She: Yes, but do you love me?

He: Move a little bit to the right. I think it will go in better. Does that feel good?

She: Mmm. (Pause) Do you love me?

He: There. Isn't that better. Oh. Oh. Wow, honey, I'm going to come.

She: Oh, that's marvelous. Oh, oh. (*pause*) Ralph...Ralph..

He: Yes?

She: Do...you...love...me?

He: Oh, I'm coming. Yes, darling. Oh, I love you.

She: (*contentedly*) I love you too.

If he says he loves her it imbues the whole scene with a sense of deep and true intimacy. Even such dubious closeness, such enforced tenderness makes her feel a little better about herself, a little bit better about being there with him. She smiles and remembers the tenderness of the past few moments. Too often the beauty, the tenderness, the spiritual union which just ensued doesn't seem to mean too much to him. For when she turns to ask him again if he loves her she finds that he has fallen asleep.

Yes, most women are ready for and capable of a mature and intimate relationship with a man. Why does a woman often find it so hard to be so close to him? Because man won't allow her to exercise her talents for honesty and openness. In the last chapter we saw how his fears of castration gave her a sword, a weapon. She is in a dilemma, hardly knowing what to do with the weapon she has been handed. And it is an awesome weapon—razor sharp— donated by men who suffer from their fears, and are desperately trying to conceal them. Give three women such a weapon and you may get three reactions.

The first woman accepts the gift, realizes its dangerous sharpness and, because she cares for the man and wants to spare him pain, decides never to acknowledge the existence of the sword. She pretends it isn't there; she disavows the gift; she tries to hide it, but as successfully as you can hide a sword behind a stool. Such women become terribly condescending, and their pity becomes more cruel, ultimately, than the quick slash might have been.

The second woman, perhaps not feeling as much affection for the man as the first woman, and feeling that she needs the sword to protect her in a male-power-struggle becomes contemptuous of the man. She rattles the saber from time to time, reminding the man that she has the power if she but chooses to use it. Such women sneer at his having given up such a protective defense in the first place. Ultimately, she makes him her slave and she becomes a princess.

The third woman simply isn't interested in the gift. She sees no need for combat, no need for saber-rattling, no need to be condescending or placating to the man by hiding the gift. Such a woman throws the sword away, feels an equality with the man and is quite sure that she can meet him on equal terms without such an unfair edge. That woman can become compatible with men; she has the best chance for ultimate intimacy with him.

The first woman makes a tactical mistake in her relationship with men. She doesn't open the doors to intimacy: she bolts them. She disenfranchises herself from any joint partnership based on equality with a man. In short, she becomes dishonest, adopts a philosophy of coddling and emerges, finally, as the *Big F*—the faker who sells herself short, and sells herself out.

Of what value is her maturity and readiness for intimacy when she disavows these and becomes dishonest? When she becomes a faker? Her knowledge of man and her insight into his needs could have been a forerunner to developing an honest relationship. Instead, she uses this knowledge in a placating manner, in her misguided efforts to be maternal and over-protective. She mistakenly feels that by sparing him from her awareness of his needs, she strengthens him.

She is aware of his often-frantic need for sex release at the expense of any spiritual closeness. She knows that he can feel he loves her but have an affair at the convention in Dallas. She knows that he may brag about his most intimate sex moments for he has a huge investment in his self-image as a Lover. She is aware of his need to be supported and she props him up and spares him from the attacks he fears. She knows how easily he can feel castrated and how important it is for him to feel intact. And again she spares him.

She knows how important muscles and athletic prowess and recognition of his intelligence are to him and she supplies him with balm in every way and keeps him from becoming fragmented. And, amazingly, she learned this when she was a little girl and one day discovered how important it was for her to watch while he jumped off the diving board or rode his bicycle without holding hands or stood in front of her flexing his muscles. He will continue to stand in front of the mirror flexing his muscles until he is an old man. And the woman will continue giving him the recognition he needs. She learned early; she learned well.

Later, as she accepts the threat she represents to man, she understands his "night out with boys" or if he is a teenager or young man his "going out with the gang." She will know that he needs his day of golf, his night at the club and his "few drinks with the boys." Men constantly gravitate towards women for relief of their sexual or nurturance needs, and then find they have to move away and seek other men's company to stabilize themselves. Why is this so? Because women are his life line to nurturance, the original umbilical cord, and the threat of cutting his manhood off at the same time. What a frightful image to behold on the one hand; what a horrible weight to carry on the other! Women know that men feel this way, and they spare them as much humiliation and degradation as possible: they try not to expose their knowledge. But again, women *do* know.

Her problems of course, and the answer to the question of why she can't have intimacy with men in spite of being so mature is that she gets sucked into *The Trap*. We called it faking. She is forced to fake her quite instinctive and intuitive responses to him on many dimensions. She fakes the very things which could produce intimacy between them: blunt honesty, straightforward openness, and refreshing candor. She fakes and takes on a pose which often presents her as naive, never too penetratingly bright, weak, dependent and childlike. Because she knows men so well she knows that to do otherwise would make him feel challenged, attacked, and highly vulnerable. There is a heavy price to be paid for such honesty and Man has proven over the centuries that he runs from such exposure.

Man is doing battle with the women, has been doing it since the beginning of time. Somewhere along the way she learned to weigh the issues, evaluate, and arrive at a pragmatic solution to the equation: the victory is a phyrric one: the battle is an exhausting one, and the threat of losing her man and destroying the relationship is a highly untenable one. Man psyched her out. He forced her to play his game. The more adept she gets at the game, the more pleased he is, for he then sees her as unchallenging, non-demanding, and non-castrating. Those spell L-O-V-E to him. He is happy. Without such threats he finds his manhood intact and she gets the final bonus for her loyalty to his masculine code of honor: a man who will stand by her and find her sexually attractive.

What a burden on the woman; to serve as a female sentinel, guarding her man's tissue-thin ego. She becomes a metaphoric athletic supporter, the jock strap for the sagging male image.

In the analysis of dreams, the purpose of the dream must be spelled out to the patient. In time, with enough dreams brought in, the symbolism and the significance of the manifest dream content are repeated enough and become clear enough to the analyst that a story unfolds. By cutting and scotch-taping the parts together, what Freud called the "gateway to the unconscious" is opened up and the analysis is meaningful and rich to both analyst and analysand. As an adjunct to analysis, dreams are crucial. But there are many ways of interpreting dreams, and one way is to apply what is known as a Gestalt technique. If the *Big F* actually got to feel like a jockstrap, and dreamed that she *was* one, I might help her analyze the dream using a Gestalt approach.

So, I had this crazy dream last night.
Oh?
Yes. I'm almost embarrassed to tell it.
(Silence on analyst's part)
I guess you want me to go on? (Pause) Well, I dreamed I was a jock strap.
(Analyst just nods)
Aren't you shocked? I am. No, of course you aren't shocked. But you never dreamed you were a jock strap, did you?
No, I can't say I have.
Well, it's a weird one, all right.
Why?

I don't know. The picture is pretty amusing, you have to admit.

Mmmmm.

Anyway, (laughing) there I was. A jock strap.

Tell me. How do you think it would feel?

How what would feel?

How do you think it would feel to be a jock strap?

Wow! I don't know. I have to think.

(silence)

I'd feel good.

Why?

I'd feel important. Isn't that silly?

No.

Yes. I'd feel important. Protective. Like if he didn't have me he'd be in trouble.

Why?

Why? Are you kidding? You're a man. You tell me what it would be like to be athletic without a jock strap.

Yes. I see what you mean.

So, if I'm a jock strap I save you...I mean..er...

You mean you save my balls.

(laughing) Yes. I hold them intact.

How else would you feel?

Like I would save you...er..from pain.

Um. Hmmmm.

And nothing really harmful could happen to you in a place where its so important. Your...

Balls.

Yes. Somehow it seems easier when we talk about it like this. I don't feel so silly.

Of course.

And there's more. I mean about being a jock strap.

Oh?

Yes. I'd feel close to the man's penis. Like I'd surround it and hold the whole thing together. Intact.

The whole thing?

Yes. The penis, the balls, they'd need me. They'd feel safe with me around. I'd have a job to do. I'd be pretty damned important, I'd think.

You certainly would.

(silence)

So, I guess that feeling is one I want, or need, right Doc? Come to think of it, I actually *have felt like that.*

Oh?

Yes. I mean I have often felt that if I wasn't careful I might hurt the poor guy somehow, and I know how damned vulnerable he is down there. I guess I'm protective of men and I guess their manhood is important to them but it is to me too.

I can understand that.

(silence)

Sometimes I think we are too damned protective of men and their Goddamned egos. They can be more flexible than we

woman give them credit for, I guess.
Flexible?
Yes.
Mmmm. Tell me, when you dream you're a jock strap, what material is the strap made of?
I never thought of that. (She thinks a moment.) Iron. That does *bear out what we've been saying, doesn't it?*
What's that?
Well, the jock strap men actually wear...
Yes?
It is, after all, elastic.

When a man ask the *Big F*: "How was it?"
She says: "It was wonderful!"
She thinks: "You are fantastic. You are spectacular. I go crazy with what you do to my body. I would like to open up once in a while, though, and ask a question or even have you ask a few questions. But I don't dare.

"I know you think a lot of the importance of sex, and of your ability in bed. I wouldn't ever want to do or say anything that would make you feel demeaned.

"Sometimes, I have orgasms and sensations I never thought were possible.

"But when I feel you are off in your own world, not a part of me, you seem like a machine, a robot. Then, I can't respond at all. I can't possibly climax at those times.

That's when I fake it. You don't know the difference. At least I hope you don't.

"How was it? When it's good, it's great. When I feel alienated from you it falls flat.

"I know you don't want to ever hear anything but what I've always told you. And you never will. After all, aren't we both on the same team? If I tell you the truth—what's in it for me?"

Women playing the *Big F* have their own act—Protector of His Manhood. How women got put into that role is one question. Whether they really ever wanted it, is another. (Remember, the patient recounting the dream said it made her—in the ultimate—feel pretty important. So there are *some* rewards to the role-playing.)

The answer to the first question is quite apparent: *men* put women into that role. How? By convincing the woman—beyond a doubt as far as she was concerned—that his tissue-thin epidermis could be stretched and finally torn by any one of her pointy fingernails. Once upon a time a woman lovingly ran the nail on her index finger down a man's back, meaning it to be but a love gesture. To her shock and dismay, he began to bleed. The choices she faced from that traumatic instant: cut her nails down so that she could lovingly run her finger down his back once again, or keep her nails intact, and run her finger along his spine, gently. Very gently. Fashion and vanity and practicality suggested she reject the first idea; security and survival allowed only for the second possibility.

Once the woman was aware of the man's hemophilic condition and as soon as she realized that antiseptic and bandage were too often inadequate to cleanse the depth of the wounds and the flow of the blood, she became protective. And who could blame her? What fun could she have with a man who was a chronic bleeder? Her course was clear. She has followed it ever since.

The second question, whether women want this role or not, is interesting. It makes a woman feel important to nurture a man, yes, but it frustrates her too. It's a heady feeling on the one hand, and a disappointing one to have to play on the other. The demands on her ingenuity are enormous, and the need to be alert and cautious are ubiquitous. What the patient who had the jock strap dream was saying was that if she could be a salving influence, a balm to his ego through her supporting him, she could enjoy it. But she pays a price: the secret code demands she try hard never to let him know she knows. That becomes her cross to bear, as well as her power and her salvation and her magnificent obsession.

She does it so brilliantly that most men don't even know it is happening. After a while the woman takes it for granted, acts her role out smoothly and easily and becomes the *Big F*...the faker who keeps non-intimacy alive.

At this point, the scripts have been assigned, and the roles are played out. She will build him up, tell him he is marvelous, get him to believe it even when she doesn't, and keep him intact in every way. She is then the Master Faker.

She tells him he's wonderful.

("Oh, honey, you're wonderful.")

She tells him he's strong and handsome.

("You're so big and strong and handsome.")

She tells him she's lucky.

("I'm so lucky to have a wonderful man like you.")

But he doesn't always feel wonderful. Sometimes he feels guilty and terribly inadequate. He doesn't feel so strong either. But since she keeps telling him he is he'll flex his muscles and expand his chest when he'd really rather let his stomach hang out and sag, and when he's feeling a little tired and would like to lie down. But if she says he's so strong and wonderful, how can he let her down?

Handsome is an ephemoral, flighty and too often fickle thing. She sees him as handsome and he sometimes takes that as a command to stay that way. He hopes he doesn't lose his hair or develop a paunch. One day he thinks he sees a receding hairline. Has she noticed? He thinks about it. Then he does what he thinks is the wise thing. He doesn't mention it.

She thinks she is lucky. A good income makes her feel lucky for she can buy things some of the other girls can't.

Did you make the sale, honey? (Or the promotion, or the bonus, or the A on the test?)

Well, no... Johnson got it.

Well, honey, he was just lucky. He'll never be one-tenth the salesman (or whatever) that you are.

Mmmm. Thanks honey. But I still feel lousy.

You'll do it, I know you can be the best. (The greatest, the smartest, the strongest, the sexiest, the handsomest, the whateverest.)

She herself doesn't always believe what she is saying. She secretly wonders how he blew the deal or goofed on the exam. "Honey, the other guy was lucky," may sound supportive. There's just one problem. Both of them wonder whether Johnson really *isn't* a better salesman. Her man, her lover, her wonderful-wonderful has an enormous number of doubts about himself. He has fears which he fears so much he won't allow himself to look at them. But she has so much faith in him that surely he isn't going to talk to her about them. After all, that would be cruel, wouldn't it, to destroy her marvelous faith and confidence in him?

So he listens to her plaudits and feels great and very lucky to have such a woman. And both side-step issues and the circling gets wider and wider as she feeds into his needs which she has adopted and made her own.

Men respond to women on all levels who lovingly play the *Big F*. Even mothers do it with their children. I knew, for example, that my mother was terribly proud of my articles in the Los Angeles *Times* and that she bragged about me to friends and family.

"My son, the future doctor," she'd write, "we are all so proud of you."

The girls I dated would let me know how impressed they were with my work at the University, and at the hospital where I was doing my internship. Especially female students at the University who would meet me at the student lounge.

"Hey, Ed," they would call out. "I hear you really cooled that Organic Chem test. Great! A lot of guys failed. It won't be long before you have that fancy office with the big waiting room and lots of patients."

They were great. Wonderful. They boosted me, and they scared the hell out of me. The more praise I received, the more frightened I became. The unspoken message I was receiving? "Don't let everyone down, buddy."

How could I let poor mom down? All those lovely and well-meaning friends? How could I tell them that there were times when I was frightened and perspiring when I took a test? How could I tell the girls I occasionally had nightmares about being thrown out? How could I tell them all that there were days I expected a call to the Dean's office saying, "Sorry, but we may have to drop you"?

Chapter 7

The Ball Breaker

The second woman we will look at accepts the sword and is crowned a princess. She may forever after be known as the Ball Breaker. She is the woman who in anger and retaliation over her ejection from the male club sets out to cut him down to size; to make him her slave.

If we recognize that she knows men so well, that she has the knowledge of male vanity, the insight into his foibles and his weaknesses, the awareness of his many fears brought on by her threats to his masculinity, we have to make an assessment: she now has the weaponry and the armamentarium to destroy him if she so wishes. Her usual opening gambit, if she takes that non-intimate road, is to attack his abilities as a provider, as a father, and as a lover. There is very little the man can retaliate with. Can he call her cold, a lousy lay? Yes. But the New Sexology and the New Education and experimentation with new sex freedoms has shown her otherwise—she can now question him for her lack of response. Can he call her a poor housewife or homemaker? Yes. But she can make him blanch, turning white at the suggestion that *he* try it for a week and then see how it feels. "Let's switch jobs, and *you* try housekeeping," is a frequent suggestion such women make. Men shrug, sometimes laugh at the idea. But it *is* a successful counter-attack on the woman's part. Can he say she is a poor mother? "How would you know," she will counter. "When are you ever around to watch?" He makes slight skin wounds with his attacks against her feminine failings; she cuts deeply when she touches on the provider-father-lover combination.

The weapon is then a complement to her major armory: her knowledge of him.

The princess isn't interested in being a housekeeper or a homemaker. Her major concern is in holding court, expecting homage, awaiting what is due her in deference to her royal lineage. If she sees herself as the Princess, then John becomes the Prince Charming, ready to supply her with the riches of the royal treasury or be prepared to die in the attempt.

The man who falls victim to the American Princess soon discovers what a drain on his pocket the demands of the royal coffers can be. He discovers that this regal woman isn't just keeping up with the Joneses. She is or wants to *be* the Joneses. She wants to create a life style which other women will envy. And such demands require an economy which is often beyond any financial goals he seeks or needs. He discovers his role is to make her achieve her standards which means to make her stand out.

This woman is so status-oriented, that job pressures on the man become enormous. He doesn't just have to get a job or lose a job. He has a way of life to achieve and preserve, and he is expected to work at it every day. The average man can find a new job; the Prince Charming has to find a new stepping-stone, a new rung on the ladder, a new success standard for his Princess.

If he fails, the penalties are devastating.

If he fails, the sword's edge is finely honed.

If he fails, the royal rage is revealed.

He'd better not fail.

The American Princess will hold back sex from the Prince Charming if she is disappointed. She will dispense her charms to the Charming or she will dispense with sexual sharing depending on whether or not he has pleased her.

Hers isn't just the headaches or the fatigue routine. The finality of her banishing him to sexual Siberia can be the withering look and his penance the withered penis.

The *Ball Breaker* is the ultimate non-intimate woman. She makes every mistake possible in helping—even forcing—the man to seek the Successful Scheme and the Impossible Dream. Hers is the ultimate rejoinder for Man's historical role in minimizing the importance of being a Woman.

Her fantasy: He should become her slave along the golden route to great success and Live for Love. Love for her and her wants.

She focuses on his fatherhood failures, reminding him whenever possible that the children's problems are the result of his weaknesses as a man and as a parent.

Career collapsibility, money management, and economic ecstasy become intertwined, and there is a shaky high wire or a trapeze which she erects from his office or his desk straight to her bed. She becomes the married prostitute; he becomes the frightened fornicator.

When a man asks the Ball Breaker, "How was it?"

She says: "It was great."

She thinks: "You are a stud. My stud. You know how to screw, I'll say that for you. You can do things which make me climb the wall. When I'm in the mood. Otherwise, you look pretty ridiculous when you try so hard, or pathetic when you whine for sex. I know you are a conceited bastard, and I wouldn't trust you as far as I could trust a boa constrictor. Sometimes when you twist into your contortions you look like a boa to me. But I have to give the devil his due. You sure know what you are doing. When I'm in the mood.

"I don't give a damn if it bugs you when I make suggestions. I'm in the bed too, you know. I have an idea or two in my head, you know.

"I don't give a damn if you do resent my asking things of you in bed you didn't think of first. I'm used to asking you for things you know. I saw a knit suit in Saks today... oh well.

"It's just too bad if those questions and demands on my part make your inadequacies pop up faster than your penis can.

"How was it? Great. So what? At least you can do *something* good. Do you want a medal or something? God knows you're a flop in enough other ways.

"I guess we'll never feel close, though. We

both come. Even together. But we never get together. Too bad. But that's the way it's going to have to be."

The Intimate Woman: Two women received the sword. Both of them were, intrinsically, quite capable of intimacy and maturity, but each handled it differently. The *Big F* decided to become placating and condescending, the *Ball Breaker* decided to become a self-crowned princess and rattle the saber from time to time as she enslaved the man in the network and the web of his own fears.

The third woman, capable of the Intimate Insight in all areas of man and woman relationships, becomes neither condescending or contemptuous. This one meets the man with a sense of equality, feels she does not need the sword and handles the dilemma of the unwanted weapon by simply throwing it away. She is the truly liberated woman, a rebel with a cause. She seeks Man's ultimate re-establishment as a man without the Sword of Damocles over his head. This *Intimate Woman* does not want to be a *Ball Breaker*. She has gone far beyond that. She simply wants to be accepted for herself.

In not stressing the accoutrements of her sex from days past—a stunning wardrobe with hair and accessories to match—she is giving the man a happy message: "You don't have to worry about money and economics with me. I don't place too much value on the material and the spangles and the floss. Just get to know me and like me for what I am. If you like the clinging vine who will "yes" you to death, I think you had better move on. I'll love you, be honest with you and lay it straight on the line. I ask you to do the same with me. And we'll both know the wonders of an honest relationship. I don't want to be the Belle of the Ball, but neither do I want to be a Ball Breaker. I just want to be a woman—to be allowed to be a total woman."

This woman does not perceive herself as one of the second class citizens of the world who has constantly been browbeaten by men. Nor does she represent that particular breed of women—so called Women's Libbers—who want to prove themselves not just equal to but better than the male. *That* woman is, essentially, totally anti-intimate and terribly non-female.

This *Intimate Woman* loves her children and can raise and enjoy them. Or not have them, if that be her choice. But her role in life is not just to see herself as a womb, a mother-object, or a vagina subject to a man's vagaries. Both sex and motherhood are of great significance to her and she can enjoy them both. But children aren't raised with a frenetic singularity of purpose or a fanatic devotion which makes the man wonder how important *he* is in the scheme of things.

A job is important. A livable and comfortable home is important. Children are important. Adequate clothing is important. And sex is the icing on the cake. But as the Greeks say, "Pan Metron Arista"—in all things, moderation.

The number of men who felt cast out, rejected, lowered in status and importance when a new child arrives is legion. Many times have I heard men tell me how they resented the attention the child got; many times have I seen a relationship and then a marriage destroyed by women who got their priorities askew and found they had raised a child and lost a lover.

The *Intimate Woman* has few images she wants to live up to. That could include not only clothes and economic super-security, but also a man's looks, the kind of work he does and his money-making capacity. The un-intimate woman has fears of stigma, the Joneses, too little education or polish or sophistication. These fears of hers become a nightmare for the man.

Oh, yes, the intimate, liberated woman does represent a challenge to the male in one huge area: his career. But she releases him from the bondage and chains in so many other areas where the un-liberated woman strangles him, that if he can get over that fear and accept her need for economic equality he'll get the promotion before she will if he deserves it, and reach his success-status-symbol if he requires it just because he is good, and can handle competition from any human being, male or female. If he can't beat out the female competition, there is plenty of male competition which will beat him out anyway. He'll have to learn to stand toe-to-toe with competition from both sexes and take his chances that his training and his skills merit the job or the promotion, and stop being so frightened that women will come better prepared than he for his job.

The *Intimate Woman* can *totally* enjoy sexual relations. She may call it "screwing," or "balling," or "loving," but if the jargon is different, her response as a female can be complete and fulfilling. She isn't going to fall into the trap of listening to other women talk of orgasms and feel she wants hers in just the traditional way. She'll enjoy. Any way she can. And if intercourse isn't quite what it should be she is ready to improvise and experiment and find other ways to enjoy sex.

Once the man knows this, once he realizes that she won't fault him for his failures and his fears, he won't feel pressured and fight back to prove himself. She can love, make love, experience love, and all that she asks of him is that he do the same. She'll use whatever armamentarium her body and mind supply. She'll ask him to do the same, knowing full well that the most erogenous zone of all is the mind. And the *Intimate Woman* has an active, groping, searching mind.

Always the pragmatist, the *Intimate Woman* sees sexual pleasure as the order of the day, not sexual performance. She doesn't demand intercourse or sex by the book, she tells the man to throw the book away, and "how to" isn't of much concern for her. She is more interested in "let's do." The time of day, the number of times a day—they mean little to her, for spontaneity is always superimposed over sex. "I feel sexy, let's make love," has more meaning to her than, "What's the matter with you, do you know how long it's been since we had sex?" or "Doesn't my big strong daddy-poo want to make love to his little lambie pie?" And it opens dimensions and doors which the unintimate woman too often never even dreamed existed.

A man asks the Intimate Woman, "How was it?"

She says what she is thinking.

"It was great. But why do you always ask? We don't have to prove anything to ourselves.

"Now you look hurt.

"I've known better moments with you; I've known worse. But the whole world doesn't revolve around sex, or my orgasm, you know.

"Fact is, you seem too intent on the whole thing a lot of times. I'd like to do more, ask more questions, tell you things I'd like you to do for me. But you seem to resent it, and you act like it's your role to take charge and act out some kind of macho thing. Sometimes I feel that if I tell you things I'd enjoy you'd wonder where I learned them.

"There's a lot about sex I don't know. Stuff I want to explore. I wish at times we could be closer so we could learn together.

"How was it?

"I loved the sex. I don't appreciate that there are times I don't feel as close to you as I would want.

"You know what? Instead of asking me 'how was it,' help me get over my occasional feelings of alienation when we make love. Then I'll feel you *really* care."

This woman won't fake anything if she can help it, be it her sex response or her intelligence. She is on her own. And she allows the man the same freedoms. He simply has the choice of meeting her in open combat or joining her in a true, honest exchange. It's a new, exciting concept. It doesn't have to have the clang of armor; it can ring with the sweet chimes of spiritual, emotional and physical intimacy.

When those bells chime, they ring the death knoll of the *Big F*, *The Ball Breaker*, and the *Sex Athlete*. It is the sound of ringing steel. The sound of the sword being thrown away.

The Reconditioning of Rapid Robert, the Robot:

What happened to Robert the Robot:

His little red light,
The one on his head,
Is blinking. Weakly.
Look! The light's gone out.

Robert, you look so weak.
Robert, your legs have stopped.
Robert, your arms don't wave any more.

Robot, robot, are you still there?
Are you still a robot?
You seem to be fading.

Robot, where are you?
And who is standing where you were?
Is it possible?
Is it... can it be...
Why, it's a real, live, human person!